# STAND UP AND BE COUNTED

# STAND UP AND BE COUNTED

Anthony Meyer

HEINEMANN : LONDON

William Heinemann Ltd
Michelin House, 81 Fulham Road, London SW3 6RB
LONDON MELBOURNE AUCKLAND

First published 1990
Copyright © Anthony Meyer 1990

The right of Anthony Meyer to be identified as author
of this work has been asserted by him in accordance
with the Copyright, Designs and Patents Act 1988.

A CIP catalogue record for this book
is available from the British Library
ISBN 0 434 46664 6

Printed in England
by Clays Ltd, St Ives plc

For Barbadee

# CONTENTS

Acknowledgements      page ix

1 Eton, Oxford, the Guards      1
1920–1944

2 The Foreign Office and the Paris Embassy      15
1945–1956

3 Moscow      28
1956–1958

4 European Stirrings      34
1958–1964

5 The Wrong Sort of Tory      45
1964–1970

6 The Breakdown of Consensus      59
1970–1979

7 The Advent of Mrs Thatcher      73
1979–1981

8 The Falklands Factor      81
1981–1982

9 The Battle for Clwyd      97
Part 1: The Triumph of Miss Brookes
1982–1983

10 The Battle for Clwyd      105
Part 2: The Rule of Law
1983

11 The Thatcher Triumph      115
1983–1987

12 Walker's Wales                                       128
   1987–1989

13 The European Fiasco                                  135
   January–June 1989

14 No One Stood Up                                      149
   July–October 1989

15 Challenge                                            158
   November–December 1989

16 Deselection and After . . .                          168
   January 1990

17 Still Very Much a Tory                               176
   1990 and Beyond

# ACKNOWLEDGEMENTS

This book is entirely my own responsibility. I do not, therefore, have to make the usual long list of acknowledgements. But I must record my thanks to my literary agent, Michael Shaw, who managed to find a publisher for it, and to Tom Weldon at Heinemann. I was lucky on my first attempt at authorship to find an editor so frank, so decisive and so perceptive.

I would like to take this opportunity to express my gratitude to my parliamentary colleagues, those who encouraged me and those who sought to discourage me in my enterprise last November – in particular to Cranley Onslow, Chairman of the 1922 Committee, Tim Renton, the Chief Whip, and George Younger, who organised the Prime Minister's campaign in the leadership election. All three showed me more kindness and courtesy than I had any right to expect.

I would also like to pay tribute to a group of people who had to put up with even more from me than did my parliamentary colleagues, namely the party workers in my constituency. For those who supported me throughout, as for those who wished to be rid of me, this has been a trying twelve months. I can only repeat what I said at the meeting in January which voted so decisively against my re-adoption; that I still regard them, all of them, as my friends and I hope they still regard me as theirs, whatever happens.

I hope so. I do know that they regard my wife as their friend. They could not do otherwise. But even they can have only an imperfect understanding of the warmth, the courage, the persistence, the wisdom and the tolerance which many times prevented me from making an even bigger fool of myself, which sustained me through what was quite an ordeal for both of us, and has given me nearly fifty marvellous years.

# CHAPTER ONE

# Eton, Oxford, the Guards

## 1920–1944

This is the story of how an obscure Tory backbencher came to challenge the most powerful Prime Minister since Churchill, the most authoritarian since Neville Chamberlain and the most durable since Lord Liverpool.

It is not an autobiography. There are already quite enough memoirs and autobiographies of really successful politicians, and at least two important ones are on the way. I shall weary the reader with only so much of my own story as is necessary to explain why I acted as I did in November 1989.

But first I need to clear up something which may puzzle the reader. Why *Sir* Anthony Meyer? What have I done to merit the award of a knighthood from my grateful leader? The answer is 'nothing'. My title is a baronetcy inherited from my grandfather, Carl Meyer, who came over from Hamburg in the 1870s, became a rich and respected financier in the City of London; and in 1910 gave the then huge sum of £70,000 to found the National Theatre. It was another sixty years before the theatre was built; but Carl Meyer's munificence brought him a baronetcy, and I am the third baronet. In my case, as Lord Melbourne remarked of the Order of the Garter, 'I like the Garter; there is no damned merit about it'.

I learned the other day to my surprise that my grandmother, who figures so sumptuously with her two children in one of Sargent's most theatrical portrait groups, and whom I recall as a terrifying *grande dame*, wrote a book in 1909 called *The Makers of our Clothes*, in which she exposed the miserable working and living conditions of the seamstresses in the East End of London who toiled to produce the elaborate satin dresses in which such as my grandmother delighted the painter's eye. I had always supposed her to be as convention-ally conservative in her views as was my father, MP for Great Yarmouth from 1925 to 1929, and my beautiful but alarming mother who ended her days happily in South Africa.

My political career began at the age of 5, carrying a banner that read 'Vote for Daddy' in the back of an open car through the streets of Great Yarmouth; it was not to be resumed for another forty-five years.

My father's victory over a well-known local Liberal bigwig was unexpected. It must have owed something to the assiduity with which he nursed the constituency; he built himself a draughty house at the end of the front and we lived there most of the time; a degree of commitment to the constituency less common in those days than now.

As a Conservative MP my father was mainly concerned to secure the repeal of the outdated and restrictive provisions of the Defence of the Realm Act, Lloyd George's attempt to curb the damage to the war effort from 'that demon, drink'. He seems to have been an orthodox, right-of-centre Conservative, as might have been expected from his background: Eton, called to the bar, distinguished service in his local territorial regiment, the Essex Yeomanry (mentioned in despatches

1915), and a steadily developing career in business (mainly centred on De Beers). He lost the Yarmouth seat in the 1929 election, and, although he was offered the safe seat of Black-pool for the 1931 election, he was by then so committed to his business activities in De Beers (of which he was the London Chairman) and other South African affairs, that he abandoned his political activity.

His involvement in South Africa meant that he and my mother were away many months in each year. For one of those years, at the age of 9, I was left in the charge of a French-Swiss governess who spoke no English; by the end of the year I was prattling away just like any French 9-year-old.

My father was a fine-looking, kind and gentle man, much less alarming than my mother; but he was as shy as I, the only child. When he was killed in a riding fall at the age of 50, and I was 15, I hardly knew him at all, though we had spent many hours riding together at Ayot St Lawrence, where we then lived (Bernard Shaw was our neighbour; he came to dinner once, but I was away at school).

Like most small boys of similar background I was sent to a preparatory boarding school, at which I was fairly unhappy for the first two years, and reasonably happy for the last three. In my early days there was a lot of bullying; it was common and approved practice for the senior boys (aged all of 13) to summon new boys to the sixth-form room and slipper them for offences such as having inky hands or sucking sweets in public.

I was even more upset by the regular baiting of boys whose appearance, voice or tastes offended their contemporaries; they would find themselves in the centre of a jeering ring of boys who repeatedly kicked them from behind. I also remem-ber feeling very sick when the headmaster decided to make an example of a singularly meek and mild boy who had committed the awful offence of buying sweets from the village shop; he caned him severely in front of the assembled school.

I did learn one valuable thing at Sandroyd. I was cast as Oberon in an open-air production of scenes from *Midsummer Night's Dream*. The eventual performance was given on a windy day on a lawn surrounded by leafy trees; and I discovered the importance of clear enunciation and of pitching your voice so that the deaf old lady in the back row can hear properly. I was also lucky enough to have one of the two or three teachers of genius that I encountered in my school career: John Graves, brother of the poet, who gave me some feel for language and a taste for literature.

In due course I became head boy, despite a formidable lack of talent for sport of any kind; but I did have a disgusting talent for acquiring and displaying knowledge, which meant that I won just about all the prizes on offer. I hope that being head boy did not make me too bossy; but I feel horribly sure that it made me unreasonably self-righteous. At least the odious practice of slippering the junior boys had been stopped by the time I got to the top of the school.

From Sandroyd I went on to Eton, to which I had won a scholarship, though a long way down the list. My father had been Captain of the Oppidans (the Oppidans or town-dwellers are those boys who are not in College, to which those who have won scholarships are entitled to go). It was therefore vaguely my ambition to follow in my father's footsteps as Captain of the Oppidans, and I eventually did so. Such records are all very well in their way; but I regret the decision not to go into College with its unique atmosphere and intellectual challenge.

At Eton there was no bullying; and although the first two

4

years had their bleak moments, the last three were almost unalloyed happiness. Up to the age of 16 I had continued to come top of every form, to win every prize. Once I had taken my School Certificate exam and become a history specialist, I sank back into the ranks of above-average performers – but I started to learn things of real value. Once again I was lucky to have a teacher of genius, a man of infinite pompousness and an even greater sense of fun; his name was John Hills. We laughed at him and with him, and he laughed at us and with us; we learned a great deal about history and even more about life.

He had been a gallant soldier and had won the MC; and on the slightest provocation would regale us with tales of his wartime experiences, so that inevitably he was called 'the man who won the war'. I still remember a note sent round by Gully Mason, a brilliant scamp who eventually got expelled after an escapade in which, heavily disguised as a military-looking uncle, he paid a visit to his housemaster to enquire how his young nephew was getting on. Gully's note ran:

> Everyone knows the man with the rose [Hills always
> wore a rose in his button hole]
> And the growth that divides his chin from his nose [he
> sported a fine black moustache]
> But it's only a few know the wonderful story
> Which accounts for that Gentleman's military glory
> So gather round chaps and prepare for the fun
> While Uncle John tells how he dealt with the Hun.
>
>  PS If you don't want to be kept in tutorial until 9 pm
> tonight for God's sake keep him off the war

Gully never did a stroke of work until his last half, when he announced that he intended to win the top history prize and very nearly did. Eighteen months later, as a sergeant rear-gunner, he was shot down and killed over Germany.

Quite apart from the history which I learned from John Hills and the German grammar drilled into us through sheer terror by a brilliant martinet by the name of Fortescue (any Etonian of my generation will blanch at the mere mention of the name, but terror is the only method of transmitting the elements of German grammar), much of what I learned at Eton was in the various societies and clubs which the boys are encouraged to form. It was in these societies that I learned to appreciate music and painting. By the end of my time, when I was something of a swell in the school, I had become Secretary of the Political Society. We had a succession of eminent statesmen to speak to us, including Lord Halifax, then Foreign Secretary, and Sir Neville Henderson, Ambassador to Germany, with whom we were about to go to war.

I have to admit that, despite the senior post which I held in the Political Society, with the opportunities which it gave for meeting these great men for dinner before the meeting, I had amazingly little real interest in politics at that time. But there was one visiting speaker who did excite me and who had a lasting effect on my outlook. Lionel Curtis, who had been one of Lord Milner's brilliant young men in South Africa, and who had had a distinguished career in the public service, was at that time working with Lord Lothian, our ambassador in Washington, to spread the ideas set out by the American journalist Clarence Streit in his book *Union Now*. This was a plea to the nations just gearing themselves up for war to accept not merely some limitation on their sovereignty, but to welcome an actual pooling of it in some kind of federal structure. At that critical stage, Curtis was thinking primarily in terms of a British–American union, but the doctrine was stated in general terms; and it is as relevant and contentious now as it was then. I freely admit that I have been sympathetic to federal ideas ever since. At a later stage in the book I shall attempt a full defence of federalism, a word as widely abused and misused as democracy itself.

I had many friends at Eton, several of whom I found again during my brief period at Oxford or later in the Brigade of Guards. With not much more than two or three exceptions, every one of them was killed in the war.

I remember a brilliant, windy day in the hills above St Vallier en Provence. My Eton housemaster, the irascible, unreasonable and strangely lovable H. K. Marsden, Bloody Bill as he was known, had taken a group of four of his pupils on a motoring holiday in France in April 1939. I can recall the exhilaration when we reached the summit, and could see the Mediterranean sparkling at our feet, smell the wild thyme and feel the breeze in our hair. There were four of us: I was the only one left alive four years later. The other three were Pip Shephard, my childhood friend and best man, Rawdon Pember, godfather to my eldest daughter, killed in the last days of the war at the Rhine crossing, and Geoffrey Dawkins, killed with his sister in the bombing of the Café de Paris in London. I mourned also the chief usher at our wedding, Francis Wigram, my wife's girlhood friend, Mike de Chair, and two other close friends from my house at Eton, John Smithers and Michael Drake. Each month brought news of a lost friend, and I grieved for them and almost more for their families, who had pinned such hopes on them.

Such sacrifices must, I suppose, be made in a cause so fundamental as the fight against Hitler's racialist Nazism; but is it really right to claim so high a price to ensure that the Union Jack, not the Argentine flag, flies over Government House in Port Stanley? It was not as if the Falkland Islanders were going to have their British way of life interfered with under nominal Argentine sovereignty. I question the right of that great Moloch, national sovereignty, to burn its children to save its pride.

While I awaited call-up for the army I had nearly a year at New College, Oxford, where I enjoyed myself hugely, and achieved rather little academically; but I did become engaged to my wife, which was more important. I was incredibly lucky with my tutors. I had Lord David Cecil with whom to discuss the plays of Shakespeare, and Isaiah Berlin to attempt, in vain I fear, to impart to me the basics of philosophy. After a couple of vacuous essays on Immanuel Kant's *Critique of Pure Reason*, the great man wisely decided that our time would be more usefully employed discussing the music of Brahms.

In April 1941 I joined the Scots Guards. After a three-month training period at Sandhurst I discovered that I did not have what it took to be a leader of men, and I have never aspired to be one. I also confirmed my own view that I would have made a competent staff officer; I think it was rather a pity that the army did not discover this in time to make me a fully fledged one. I learned something else at Sandhurst; I came under the direction for drill purposes of Regimental Sergeant Major Lord, surely one of the finest warrant officers which the British Army has ever produced. What he taught his squad of somewhat self-important cadets was that even so basically brainless an occupation as square-bashing can bring not just satisfaction but real exhilaration if it is done well enough; and as we swung onto the passing-out parade square to the strains of 'Stars and Stripes for Ever' we felt we could burst with pride. As George Herbert put it;

A servant with this clause makes drudgery divine,
Who sweeps a room as for thy laws makes that and the
action fine.

Later in the war RSM Lord was captured and held in a prisoner-of-war camp in Germany. Conditions in those camps had become truly dreadful in the closing stages of the war; food, clothing, heat were running out, and in many camps morale and discipline had collapsed altogether. But, as the first advance troups of the Allied armies entered the camp where RSM Lord was held, they found the men smartly drawn up on parade, their boots polished, their trousers pressed and a look of confidence and determination on every face.

My closest companion at Sandhurst, as he had been at Eton and New College, was the brilliant, maddening Victor Gordon Ives, unreasonably gifted as academic, satirist, painter and poet. Had he not been killed at Anzio he would have been, without any doubt, one of the outstanding men of his generation in whatever field he had chosen to excel. I still remember the lyrics which he wrote for the passing-out concert for our company at Sandhurst. I should explain that although we cadets used to spend most Saturday evenings in London's West End, in theory we were allowed to go out to dinner only within the boundaries of the Aldershot Command, and we were required to state on the 'Dining Out Sheet' the town of our destination. I should also explain that our delightful squad instructor, the champion golfer Gerry Micklem, bore an uncanny resemblance to Leslie Henson, then starring in *Up and Doing* at the Saville Theatre. Part of Victor's lyric ran as follows:

> Aldershot, Bagshot, Camberley and Fleet
> These are the names on the Dining Out Sheet
> Farnborough, Farnham, Crowthorne and Yately
> Are some of the places we've visited lately.
> The Aldershot Command is most elastic

There's nothing you can't find there if you try;
The best tailor, the best hatter
The best bars in which to chatter
Leslie Henson, Phyllis Robins, Frances Day.
The other day we went to *Up and Doing*
A show in Farnham that is quite the rage
And imagine our surprise
When, without the least disguise
We all saw Gerry Micklem on the stage.

Alas, the passing-out parade lived up to its name, and the audience was far too drunk and disorderly even to listen to Victor and me and a couple of other cadets giving a highly polished rendering of these lyrics.

Why did I join the *Scots* Guards, when I have not a drop of Scots blood in my veins? The explanation is that most of my friends had joined that regiment – many of them no more Scottish than I. More to the point, why were they ready to have me? Frankly I do not know; but after a short period of ritual humiliation deliberately inflicted on all young officers by a group of embittered and militarily useless majors (we, new young officers, were solemnly told that 'officers in the Brigade of Guards wear moustaches', whereupon, I am glad to say, the only one among us who had a moustache promptly shaved it off), I was happy in the company of my genuinely Scottish brother officers. I was likely to be happy in any case, since I was just and blissfully married.

The Brigade of Guards and its ethos buried, for the time being, any unconventional ideas I might have had about the unacceptability of war, or about the need for some fresh thinking on the future of the nation state. I was now a good, safe, sound Tory; and I earned the admiration of my superior officers by the eloquence with which I defended the role of the

House of Lords during a session of the Army Bureau of Current Affairs.

After the odious Training Battalion at Pirbright, and a brief stay in the Tower of London, taking turns to mount the Guard at Buckingham Palace, and entertaining our friends at the officers' mess in St James's Palace, I was posted to the 4th battalion, at that time under some very damp canvas near Frome. There then ensued a process which will be familiar to all who know the armed services. Brigade Headquarters rings up the adjutant: 'We need a liaison officer [a sort of unpaid, unskilled junior staff officer]. Send us your best man.' The adjutant looks around for his least valuable officer. In this case the choice was obvious; and I was posted to Brigade Headquarters. Life there was almost sheer delight, with rumbustious after-dinner sing-songs, very little work, and quite a lot of time to spend with my wife, who had found a room nearby. A few months of this idyllic existence, and Divisional Headquarters rang up: 'We want a new liaison officer. Send us your best man . . .' And so I found myself at Divisional HQ: not quite so intimate or cosy, but enjoyable too in its way; and it was at Divisional HQ, of the Guards Armoured Division, that I was to end my military career some eighteen months later.

But before that I was given the opportunity to show that I could do a good job as a staff officer. My lowly function was as assistant to the General Staff Officer, Grade III in charge of Training. In April 1943 a particularly virulent strain of jaundice swept through Guards Armoured Division HQ, and I was the only one of six officers on the 'G' side of the HQ to escape the virus (I had caught it and recovered two years earlier, while working on bomb sites during the blitz in London). For nearly six weeks I ran the whole of that part of Divisional HQ single-handed; and, although it meant about sixteen hours a day seven days a week, I managed to keep the show on the road. Shortly afterwards King George VI and Queen Elizabeth (now the Queen Mother) came to visit our HQ, and I was singled out for special praise by the, as ever, tongue-tied King; and the Queen, on the spot as ever, enquired very closely after my daughter Carolyn born a month earlier.

The Guards Armoured Division moved restlessly around the United Kingdom, from Somerset to Norfolk to East Yorkshire to the south coast as we prepared for the long-delayed invasion of northern France. Meanwhile, other Guards regiments were fighting in North Africa or Italy; and almost each month brought news of the death in action of another of my, or my wife's friends. *We* were preparing for an opposed landing on the highly fortified coast of northern France, an operation which most of us in our hearts knew to be unfeasible. But now I, and many others, learned another lesson. General Montgomery, fresh from his triumph at El Alamein, had been appointed to take charge of the British forces assigned to Operation Overlord. He made it his business during the first few months of 1944 to address as many officers and men of the invasion force as could be assembled in the time; and he infected every single one of them with his determination and his boundless self-confidence. I discovered what the term 'morale-boosting' really meant; and I learned to give proper weight to that quality of leadership, to which I make no claim for myself, but which I salute when I see it in others. And let me say straight away that I very readily concede that Margaret Thatcher has this quality, this shining quality, in superabundance.

We eventually set sail from London Docks, where the towers of Canary Wharf are now rising, on Derby Day, 1944. There was a carnival atmosphere among the officers on board as we sailed down the Thames with the wireless blaring out the Derby commentary from Newmarket (where it was run during the war years). We hugged the coast of Kent that night, and awoke the next morning to the amazing spectacle of the sea lane from the Isle of Wight to the French coast, half a mile wide and eighty miles long, crowded with shipping in both directions, with barrage balloons moored every few hundred yards to keep German fighters at a respectful distance. By tea-time we dropped anchor a mile off the French coast, and prepared to disembark. A large raft was brought alongside, and our vehicles, with all our worldly possessions loaded into them, were swung over the ship's side onto the raft. At this moment the wind began to blow. Within minutes we were in a full storm, and the raft swung wildly. Before long the ropes started to fray; within an hour the raft had broken loose, and we waved farewell as it and all our possessions were swept from our sight towards the surf beating on the shore. It was clear that we were going to have a very uncomfortable war. We had four days of that storm. We did, after a day or two, get over our seasickness despite the diet of plum pudding and spam which we had for every meal, being the only rations on board.

Eventually the wind died down, and we were able to land, in amphibious vehicles this time. It was an emotional moment for me to land on French soil; it was an even more joyful moment for all of us to find our lost vehicles safely parked in Canadian Corps car park, with their precious contents intact; and we toasted our incredible good fortune with a bottle of champagne which Aylmer Tryon, the General's ADC, had been sent by an aunt in Australia. Afterwards we felt able to forgive Aylmer even his endless reminders, as we had lain storm tossed, that 'Worse things happen at sea'.

I cannot claim any deeds of great glory in the conflict. On the night before we set sail from London I had mislaid my only weapon, a very cumbrous revolver, in the scramble to dodge the V1s (buzz bombs) which were exploding around us in the docks. Just as well, as I should have been unlikely to hit anything with it except my foot. I did, however, make one notable contribution to the winning of the war. I had been assigned to what was known as the Command Post: a small group of officers, drivers, tanks and armoured cars accompanying the Divisional Commander, the diminutive but heroic General Alan Adair, very close behind the front line of advancing troups as we attempted, in vain, to break through the German anti-tank screen near Caen on 18 July 1944. My place was in a fearsome-looking Sherman tank, whose gun had been replaced by a dummy, but which was equipped for communication with Corps Headquarters. Suddenly my earphones crackled: 'This is the Corps Commander; I am coming to see you. Where are you?' I hastily consulted the map, worked out the exact location, encoded it, and sent it off. I reckoned that General O'Connor would be with us in ten minutes. Ten minutes later two things happened simultaneously. The Germans found our position, and dropped an almighty barrage of high explosives on us. We cowered safely behind our armoured turrets, battened down. My radio crackled again: 'This is General O'Connor. I have been to the map reference you gave me and you're ****** not there. Where the ****** are you?' Ten minutes later still, the bombardment had died down and a very testy Corps Commander arrived in a totally unarmoured jeep. To his dying day he never knew that he owed his life to my poor map-reading.

Four days later my war ended abruptly. We had been halted by mud and by German anti-tank weapons which had survived the most ferocious RAF bombing. I was in a rather lightly armoured communications vehicle when there was a very loud bang, followed by a good deal of daylight pouring in through the roof, and an awful lot of blood on the table beside me, which turned out to be my own.

# CHAPTER TWO

# The Foreign Office and the Paris Embassy

## 1945–1956

For some days I hovered between life and death in a field hospital in Normandy. Brother officers who called to see how I was had written me off, and were at a loss what messages to send to my wife, expecting her second baby in a month and desperate for news at home. However, I got back in one piece, only to relapse badly just as our son was about to be born. All in all it was eight months before I could be let out of hospital on a short lead. I did a lot of reading, and even got a very rudimentary grasp of economics; but I cannot claim that my involvement in politics started from then. I do, however, remember being horrified by an RAF bomber pilot visiting a friend in hospital at Midhurst and boasting that, if he had any spare bombs on the return run, he would drop them on the most easily identifiable school. I also remember how impressed I was by the Bishop of Chichester, Dr Bell, who made a lone stand against the continued bombing of an already prostrate Germany. It was the authentic voice of Christian compassion; and it aroused the same hostility and scorn as do the pleas of the present Archbishop of Canterbury, Dr Runcie, for a national and international reconciliation.

When I finally got out of hospital, just in time to witness the London celebrations of VE day, I was anxious to find a job. The trouble was that my wound kept blowing up at least once a year for the next four years. I had no qualifications, a very utilitarian degree, and no commercial experience. However, the Civil Service were anxious to employ anyone they could lay their hands on, and through my father-in-law's connections I got a temporary job in the Treasury, winding up the affairs of the Polish Government in exile in London (for Churchill and Stalin had agreed to recognise the Soviet stooge government in Warsaw). I came to know a number of Poles and found them immensely attractive.

After a year in the Treasury I took the Civil Service entrance exam, which consisted mainly of a series of tests held at a country house party in Surrey. I was aiming at the Home Civil Service; but a perceptive member of the staff advised me (having just met my wife, who had to come each day to dress my wounds) that I, and she, would be better suited to the Foreign Service. And so it was. I had four years in the Northern Department of the Foreign Office, dealing with Poland, and then Czechoslovakia. I learned a lot about Communist take-over methods, for that was the period of the Communist 1948 *coup d'état* in Prague and the gradual ousting of the remaining moderates from the Russian-imposed government in Warsaw.

By 1951 the Foreign Office decided that it could send me abroad without running an unacceptable risk of my falling ill again and costing the Service huge sums in foreign doctors' bills; so in September 1951 I was posted to Paris.

I had the fantastic luck to stay five years in Paris. My wife and I worked hard and we played hard, and both were equally enjoyable. We got to know very many French people in all walks of life; indeed, very little of our time was spent with our own compatriots. We fell in love with Paris and with France; and we have remained in love with both ever since.

We seemed to meet pretty well all the famous people at that time: Albert Schweitzer, T. S. Eliot, Graham Sutherland, Billy Graham, John Gielgud, Yehudi Menuhin, Charlie Chaplin, Maurice Chevalier, Marcel Pagnol, Albert Camus. We went to the most amazing parties, many of them given by the Marquis de Cuevas, who was keen to impress our fey and very Welsh Ambassadress, Maudie Harvey, and would bring his entire *corps de ballet* plus Rosella Hightower and full orchestra to Embassy receptions; fancy-dress balls at Vaux le Vicomte, Biarritz, the Hameau at Versailles. I treasure one memory: Nancy Mitford, who set out to be more French than the French and was always prefectly dressed by, I think, Jacques Fath, walking down the long Embassy garden arm in arm with Louise de Vilmorin (authoress of *Madame de*, and friend and subsequently wife of André Malraux), who set out to be more English than the English, dressed in tweeds, twin sets, pearls and brogue shoes. At three hundred yards there was no possibility of confusing them, Nancy stumping along in her four-inch heels, as unmistakeably English as a suet pudding; and Louise mincing delicately, unmistakeably French in her clodhoppers and tweeds.

A pleasant anecdote from this time concerns the then Papal Nuncio, Cardinal Roncalli (later the much beloved Pope Paul XXII). By convention the Papal Nuncio is the doyen of the Corps Diplomatique in Paris; and Cardinal Roncalli like his predecessors had perforce to attend many public occasions, secular as well as sacred. Someone asked this saintly man, 'Your Eminence, do you not find it hard sometimes to reconcile your holy calling with the worldly activities in which you are obliged to take part?' To which the Cardinal replied, 'Not really; I enjoy everything I do, for I am a happy man. But there is one thing that does occasionally bother me. When I find myself sitting next to a lady whose dress is cut just a little too low in front, or a little too tight at the back, I find that people are staring, not at her, but at me'.

But, for the reader of this book, there is only one matter that is relevant. Almost my first duty on arrival at the Embassy was to accompany the Minister, the brilliant William Hayter, to the negotiations at the French Foreign Ministry, the Quai d'Orsay, for the setting up of the European Defence Community (EDC).

The EDC was designed to be the second stage in that process of integration in Western Europe which had begun five years earlier with the European Coal and Steel Community (ECSC), the so-called Schuman Plan. There was the added factor that the Americans were getting increasingly concerned about the growing evidence of Soviet aggressive intentions, and were desperately anxious to get the West Germans to contribute to the defence of the West. But the French would not hear of this unless the German forces were in some way integrated with other Western forces so as to be incapable of independent action; and unless there was a firm British commitment to participate in the process.

Churchill, back in power after his rejection by the voters in 1945, was pretty scornful of what he called 'this sludgy amalgam' of a European Army; but he was basically well disposed to the process of European integration, while being a bit equivocal about the extent of British involvement. But Eden, his Foreign Secretary and successor designate, seemed to have almost as highly developed an antipathy to European integration as Margaret Thatcher. The French, and the Germans too, were desperately anxious that Britain should join the EDC, even on such terms as we might demand; but Eden would have none of it.

The Treaty was signed in great pomp in the historic Salon de l'Horloge at the Quai d'Orsay, but it was never ratified. Pierre Mendes France, who had come to power in France to terminate the endless war in Indo-China, and who aroused the same sort of fierce hatreds and loyalties as Jack Kennedy, was then, and remained, a sceptic about European unity. As Prime Minister it was his task to get the French National Assembly to ratify the European Defence Community Treaty; but the Assembly did not want German rearmament, and certainly not without the reassuring presence of the British. I feel pretty sure that Mendes France could have won over the Assembly had he really wanted to; but he made no effort. For one young British admirer watching the all-night sitting from the diplomatic box it was one of the saddest nights of his career.

The most distasteful feature of this incident was the unholy alliance between the Communists (the French Communists were then, and long remained, firm Stalinists) and the ultra-nationalists of the Gaullist right. But the alliance between extreme right and extreme left against any kind of international co-operation was not new; it is still very much a factor today, and not only in France.

French failure to ratify the EDC Treaty removed none of the urgency of the need for German rearmament. Eden now showed himself at his best, and in a few short months had cobbled together the London and Paris Agreements, which set up the Western European Union (WEU), providing a framework to contain and limit German rearmament. The process was not without its difficulties, and the British Government had in the end to give specific guarantees to maintain a level of British forces on the Continent; guarantees which, had they been given four months earlier, would have saved the EDC.

One memory of those hectic days comes back very vividly. Eden, accompanied by his Defence Secretary, Harold Macmillan, had returned to the Embassy from an extremely uncomfortable meeting with Mendes France at which Mendes had been able to produce a document, unknown to Eden, which contained a British pledge to back France's claim to the Saar. Eden was already a sick man, and his temper was notorious. As he came up the Embassy steps he cursed everybody in sight; the footman who opened the door, the maid who took his coat, his Private Secretary to whom he handed his papers, the Ambassador's housekeeper who enquired whether he wanted tea. Ten paces behind came Harold Macmillan, dispensing a cheery or comforting word to all and sundry, 'My dear fellow, how's the wife?', 'I do hope your rheumatism is better today', and so on, all the way up the curving Embassy staircase.

Half-way through my five years in Paris Oliver Harvey, awkward, crusty, detesting publicity and music almost equally, but with a deep knowledge and love of France, was replaced by Gladwyn Jebb, a much more flamboyant figure. Gladwyn had many enemies at the time; and he could be alarming to those who showed any fear of him. I found him one of the best chiefs I ever worked for; he may have been trying as a subordinate or even as a colleague; but as a boss he was terrific. He would give his staff plenty of discretion and nearly always back their judgement once he had assessed its value. Gladwyn was one of the first British officials to appreciate the seriousness, the rightness and the inevitability of the moves towards European unity which resumed quite soon after the failure of the EDC.

My job in the Embassy was to report on French internal affairs; and I found myself getting closely involved, almost too closely involved, in the French political scene. I used to attend many sittings of the French National Assembly, often all-night sittings, and both my wife and I developed close friendships with politicians of all parties.

The political grouping whose ideas I found most attractive was the Mouvement Republicain Populaire (MRP), the centrist, Catholic, and strongly pro-European party which was the sheet-anchor of the succession of shifting coalitions which provided France's seemingly endless procession of governments under the Fourth Republic. However, although this was the party whose ideas corresponded most closely, not only to my own, but also to the attitude of the British Government, I found it strangely difficult to warm to any of their members; though it was impossible to withhold admiration, even affectionate admiration, from the saintly Robert Schuman, one of the father-figures of European unity. I remember deriving a certain mischievous pleasure from introducing this devout Catholic at a party at the British Embassy to Billy Graham, and having some problem in finding the French equivalent for a 'hot gospeller'.

I found it easier to warm to individual Gaullists, even though I disliked their shrill nationalism; and to some of the Socialists, though I disliked some of their economic doctrines, and their obsessional hatred of the Catholic schools.

One of our dearest friends among French MPs was a Conservative of the old school, Jacques Bardoux. He had written a life of Queen Victoria, and was an expert on British nineteenth-century history. He had all the elaborate courtesy of the *ancien régime*. He was also the grandfather of an even better known French politician, Valery Giscard d'Estaing. Some years later, when I first met Giscard at the French Embassy in London on the occasion of his state visit, I told him that I had had the honour of knowing his grandfather. 'So did everyone else', was the reply. I can understand how even Mrs Thatcher found him somewhat arrogant; though I am told that, like Dr David Owen, he has now developed an unexpected streak of humility.

French governments came and went like the seasons; and each collapse seemed to follow a major scandal. Yet the economy of France forged steadily ahead. There was a saying curent at the time, 'France, in total disarray, moves steadily upwards; Britain, in perfect order, subsides beneath the waves'. The key lay in the work of Jean Monnet and his planners. Monnet was not only the father of European unity, he was also the author of French recovery. I would be prepared to argue that Monnet was the greatest man of our century, greater than either Churchill or de Gaulle. But he has never received his due recognition in this country, understandably perhaps, in view of his ability to put nationalism in its true perspective. I was very happy, at Question Time in the House of Commons one day, to be able to put the Prime Minister in the position of being obliged to pay a tribute to this greatest of Frenchmen and greatest of Europeans.

But, at the time that I was in Paris, the British Government was still pursuing the mirage of a European Free Trade Area closely tied in with the USA; a concept which was widely regarded on the Continent as being intended more to sabotage their efforts to move towards integration than as a real step towards closer co-operation. Gladwyn was very staunch then, as he has been ever since, in upholding the concept of real integration in Europe and of full British involvement in that process. It did little to enhance his popularity with the Foreign Office establishment, which was still a long way from being converted to the European cause (this did not happen until 1961, and lasted up to the last few years).

Towards the end of my stay in Paris, in 1956, it was becoming increasingly apparent that the Fourth Republic could not go on much longer. The endless procession of unstable coalition governments did not provide the assurance of stability and continuity necessary to tackle the urgent problems of Indo-China and French North Africa. The air was full of the most improbable rumours of *coups d'états* by the most unlikely characters. There was only one credible challenger to the regime, General de Gaulle, who, having incarnated French refusal to surrender in 1940, and having returned to France as liberator and head of a provisional government in 1944, had stalked out in fury in 1947 because of the shifts and compromises to which he had been obliged to resort in framing the constitution of the Fourth Republic. He retreated to his native village of Colombey les deux Eglises, and poured anathema on the institutions he so abominated. Because of his refusal to accept the legitimacy of the regime the British Embassy, accredited as it was to the President of the Republic, could have no official contact with him. Harold Macmillan, building on their wartime association in Algiers, had been to see him once very privately; it had not been a rewarding encounter.

It seemed to me that the demise of the Fourth Republic was so imminent that we in the Embassy should make some attempt at any rate to open a line of communication. I had a number of friends who were on his staff, and one of them, Diomède Catroux, arranged for me to see that great man. I had, of course, to get clearance from the Ambassador. He, very wisely, decided that if the Foreign Office was consulted they would say 'no'; so he told me not to ask silly questions and to get on with it.

I was given an appointment to see the General in his party offices in the Rue de Solferino; I was not to find another set of political party offices so shabby and dilapidated until I encountered the offices of the Clwyd North West Conservative Association in Colwyn Bay.

De Gaulle received me most graciously, showing no sign of irritation at being pestered by so junior an official. He treated me to a lengthy monologue in his majestic French on the iniquities of the existing, absurd constitution, and the impossibility of any man of real value (and he conceded that there were men of value trying to do their best) being able to make an effective contribution to public life so long as it remained in force. As for him, he had had enough of battering his head against a stone wall; it was for others to try to mend matters. He certainly had no intention of re-entering the fray.

After half an hour of this I considered that I had taken up enough of the great man's time; and I rose to leave. I thought that I should try to end the conversation (well, it was hardly a conversation) on a pleasant note. So I thanked him for his magisterial, if gloomy account, and then added brightly, 'Perhaps, mon Géneral, I may have the good fortune to be posted back to Paris in twenty years, and find that there has been an improvement'. To which the General retorted, 'Come back in a hundred years'.

He gave no indication that he might be ready to return to active politics; indeed, he seemed to convey the impression that he would refuse to be drafted to office. And yet, within two years he was swept back into power on a tide of nationalist hysteria fuelled by the failure of France's campaign against Algerian independence.

As everyone knows, de Gaulle's first act on returning to power was to accord independence to Algeria; and to crush the plotters on the extreme right who had supported him in the mistaken belief that he would keep Algeria under French rule.

De Gaulle was, indeed, a man of paradoxes: an authoritarian with a strict regard for civil liberty; a potential dictator with democratic scruples. He had a deep love of France; and an equally deep contempt for the French. His stiffness and seeming arrogance were notorious, and had driven Churchill to distraction during the war. But he himself had a good explanation: 'I was so weak', he wrote, 'that, had I bent ever so slightly under the huge burden I was carrying, I would have collapsed'.

During his ten-year rule, from 1958 to 1968, de Gaulle restored French self-confidence and provided a stable political framework for a further economic leap forward. As an old-fashioned nationalist he disliked the supranational aspects of the European Economic Community to which France had subscribed a few months before he came to power; but he was enough of a realist to recognise the benefits which the EEC could bring to France, and he contented himself with emasculating the powers of the supranational elements in the EEC, notably the Commission and the Parliament. De Gaulle might have destroyed the Community by taking France out of it; but he did cripple its development for even longer than the ten years of his presidency by shifting the emphasis away from common action and towards horse-trading between national states, each clinging grimly to every shred of its sovereignty. Harold Macmillan was wont to say that his friend de Gaulle (he always retained some affectionate regard for him) had done more damage to Europe than Hitler.

During the ten years of de Gaulle's presidency his authority was so unchallenged that French politics went into hibernation. At the end of ten years the silence was rudely broken by the student riots of May 1968. De Gaulle realised that he had lost touch with the deep feelings of the French people; and that he did not have the adaptability to restore social harmony. Knowing that he was out of touch and that from now on it would be downhill all the way, he withdrew from the scene, and handed over to a successor who could better defend the ideas which were so precious to him and so indispensable to France. Lucky France, to have had so worthy a successor available in the person of President Pompidou; luckier still to have had a chief who knew when it was time to go!

All good things must come to an end. I had contrived to extend my stay in Paris well beyond the normal two years through the skilful exploitation of a lucky accident. When Oliver Harvey retired in 1953, the Minister at the Embassy, William Hayter, was appointed Ambassador in Moscow, and the Head of Chancery, John Beith, was also promoted. So I went to see the incoming Ambassador, Gladwyn Jebb, and I said to him, 'You have just arrived; you are losing your Minister and your Head of Chancery. You are going to need someone to provide continuity. I am ready to sacrifice myself for this worthwhile cause'. And he took the bait. I had already managed to impress him, because one of the first people he wanted to meet on his arrival was François Mitterrand, then a rising star on the non-socialist centre left. I knew a good many French politicians, but not Mitterrand. There was no point in admitting that. So I just said, 'Oh yes, I'll get him round to lunch next week', rang Mitterrand's office, told him the Ambassador was keen to meet him, and we had lunch à trois the following week.

I was able to study François Mitterrand quite closely at that time; I even attended one of his election meetings at a primary school in his constituency in central France. He struck me then as being almost too devious even for French politics; but he was an impressive speaker, and he was certainly no socialist.

One phenomenon which occurred during my last months in Paris was the sudden rise to prominence of Pierre Poujade and his followers. Poujade was a little man with a big mouth; but his appeal to lower middle-class resentment against the liberal consensus which had dominated French politics since the Liberation filled me with some foreboding. Poujadism was neither fascism, nor a precursor of Thatcherism; but there is something disquieting about the appeal to anti-foreigner, anti-establishment resentment which is a factor in all three.

By 1956 my number was up. I was due to be posted elsewhere. It was to be Moscow. I didn't think I was going to enjoy it. I was right.

# CHAPTER THREE

# Moscow

## 1956–1958

I set sail from Surrey Docks for Leningrad in the good ship *Molotov*, on 30 October 1956. It was the day on which the Anglo-French ultimatum to Egypt to withdraw from the Suez Canal was due to expire. The Russian tanks were rumbling through the streets of Budapest, extinguishing any hopes of Communism with a human face. My wife was on the quayside; she was planning to join me three months later, when I would be able to take possession of one of the Embassy's stock of flats in Moscow. On board was half the Bolshoi Corps de Ballet, and Derek Thomas, then about to take up his first foreign posting and now one of the Foreign Office's most distinguished mandarins, with his Dutch wife Lineka.

The North Sea lived up to its reputation. The decor on the *Molotov* was entirely green and orange plush. Breakfast was apt to consist of red caviar and a strange stew of meatballs in grey gravy called 'Fritters with Pitters'. We were all very sick. As we lay in our cabins we were solaced by the ship's intercom (which could not be switched off) giving a twenty-four hour commentary in Russian (of which I had by then acquired a smattering) about the *Angliski-Franzoski-Israelski aggressori*; and about the fraternal help which the heroic Red Army was giving to the people of Hungary threatened by fascist counter-revolution.

When the ship put in to Stockholm for a couple of hours I made a dash for the British Embassy. The Ambassador was my old chief from the Northern Department of the Foreign Office, Robin Hankey. 'For God's sake, what are we to tell these Russians? What on earth are we doing in Egypt while the Russians are getting away literally with murder in Hungary?' Robin ruminated. 'Do tell me about the last few months in Paris; it must have been fascinating.' So I left, none the wiser nor better armed to withstand the propaganda barrage.

From Leningrad to Moscow we travelled on one of those spendidly antique broad-gauge leisurely Russian trains, unchanged since Tolstoy's days. As we drove up to the gates of the Embassy, on the banks of the Moscow River facing the Kremlin wall, a large crowd was massed around the gates. This was a 'spontaneous' demonstration against the Suez operation; the demonstrators, it turned out, had been given the afternoon off from their factory work and ordered to put on a convincing demo.

Once inside the Embassy I was taken upstairs for a glass of sherry with the Ambassador, my former superior officer in Paris, William Hayter. I was not quite sure what he was angriest about: the manifest connivance of the police in the crowd's invasion of the Embassy grounds; or the crass folly of the British Government's involvement in the Suez adventure. He was in the middle of a telephone call from the US Ambassador, the great 'Chip' Bohlen. The US administration had made clear their disapproval, indeed their outright hostility to Eden's Suez operation. But despite this what counted above all in Moscow in those days, and ever since, up to the advent of the new Gorbachev dawn, was Western solidarity. 'I hear, William, that you're having a small problem. I'm just getting my Cadillac round and I'll be over your way with the Stars and Stripes flying in twenty minutes'. 'Very kind of you, Chip, but I don't think Foster Dulles would like that much'.

In the end the gesture proved unnecessary; the spontaneous demonstration ceased promptly at factory closing time and the crowd drifted off, commenting approvingly on the Embassy flower-beds.

But life in Moscow became pretty dour. It was sad for those who had been *en poste* for a few months, as there had been a very notable thawing in relationships, and more and more private citizens were beginning to pluck up the courage to talk to foreigners. Now the cold war resumed in earnest. All contact with foreigners was strictly forbidden. Foreigners, and especially Western diplomats, were spied on; their telephones were tapped, they were followed everywhere, and their servants were trained as KGB spies. It was an intensely disagreeable atmosphere, especially for me, who in Paris had spent far more of my time among French people than among my own compatriots or other diplomats.

Not that the KGB surveillance was especially clever. There was a pleasant story of two Western diplomats who went with their wives to stay the weekend at the Astoria in Leningrad, the most old-fashioned, and thus the best hotel in the Soviet Union. They were allotted adjoining rooms, both of which had a balcony giving on to St Isaac's Cathedral. When they met for breakfast downstairs, the Smiths said to the Browns, 'Did you sleep well?' 'We didn't sleep a wink', came the reply. 'You snored like chain saws all night.' 'How do you like that?' retorted the Smiths. 'It was *you* snoring all night who kept *us* awake.'

Very mysterious. Next evening they went out on the balcony
to admire the view. Then they noticed that between their two
adjoining rooms there was a little door, like a shed door. They
pushed it in. There, wedged into a narrow slit between their
rooms was a little old man, fast asleep and snoring loudly. It
is hard to believe that his report to the KGB on the conver-
sations which he had overheard from his listening post can
have been of very great value.

I learned one enduring lesson in Moscow; a lesson which
influenced the rest of my career in public life. It is that
socialism, however admirable in theory, cannot be used as a
means of governing a country without unacceptable mutila-
tion of human nature. Of course one has to make allowance
for the character of the Russian people, who, despite their
great gifts, are allergic to all kinds of organisation and most
kinds of work. But the truth remains, or at least it remains
valid for me, that Socialism runs against the grain of human
nature; and that the art of government is to go with the grain
of man's desire to better himself, to compete with his fellows
and to provide for his family.

Nowhere is this fundamental incompatibility more evident
than in agriculture. The failure of pretty well every socialist
regime to produce enough food to feed its people has been
universal and spectacular. Countries which once exported
their agricultural products to the world, like Burma or
Romania, have been reduced to begging for food for their
peoples as a result of trying to apply socialism to farming.
This is not a justification for applying unrestricted free-market
mechanisms to agriculture; it is also vital to give the worker
on the land a feeling of proprietorship. But it is an argument
for a mixed economy, in agriculture as in everything else.

The other, equally enduring lesson I learned was the persistence and the virulence of nationalism in its most assertive

form, even among, perhaps especially among, a people who had paid lip service to internationalism for more than forty years. Although there were many of us in the Embassy who shared the Ambassador's deep concern about the Suez operation, I never met a single Russian who had the slightest qualms about the far more dreadful things the Russians were doing in Hungary.

I was supposed to be the Commercial Secretary. It mainly involved fixing up meetings between visiting British businessmen and Soviet trade officials; in practice, it meant trying to cheer them up as they waited day after day for an appointment. It was not a very satisfying job, and I was not very good at it.

There were consolations, of course. The theatre was excellent; the ballet, and less surely the opera, were outstanding. There was skiing of a sort on the steepish banks of the Moscow River. There were occasional trips. When my wife joined me, we were able to get to Leningrad, which is everything it is cracked up to be; and to Kiev, Odessa and Kishinov in Moldavia.

When my wife had to return to England to look after her very sick father, I got increasingly bored, and careless. As I was walking home after a dinner party one night, a car drew up beside me and a woman said, 'I have a very urgent message for you; get in'. And I got in. At the same moment the door opened on the other side of the car, and a militia man was there. 'Your papers, please'. I had walked straight into the oldest trap of all.

There was no security lapse; I went straight to tell the Ambassador (by this time it was the benign Patrick Reilly, who had followed William Hayter first as Minister in Paris, and then as Ambassador in Moscow). But I had been inexcusably careless. Quite rightly the Foreign Office decided that it was no longer safe to leave me in Moscow and recalled me a few weeks later. I don't know how I would have got through those few weeks without the friendship and support of Alan Urwick, then a junior secretary at the Moscow Embassy, now, after a distinguished Ambassadorial career, Serjeant at Arms in the House of Commons with the ultimate responsibility to arrest me if I try the Speaker's patience beyond endurance (not easily done with the present Speaker).

# CHAPTER FOUR

# European Stirrings

## 1958–1964

Back to the Foreign Office and a well deserved reprimand. Thereafter a spell in the Economic Relations Department where, frankly, I don't think I contributed much of value, and six months unpaid leave in which I learned to ski quite well. My wife and I travelled a good deal, including a visit to South Africa to visit my mother, a visit which confirmed all my worst expectations about the white way of life in that country. After that I was posted to the Western Organisations Department. This was most congenial, and I worked under a succession of very able Heads of Department and Under-Secretaries.

I was not in fact directly involved in the British negotiations in 1960–1 for entry into the EEC; though from time to time I find myself half-suggesting that I was, rather like the Prince Regent who fondly imagined that he had fought in the Battle of Waterloo, and would say to the Duke of Wellington in front of his courtiers, 'That's right, Wellington, isn't it; I was at Waterloo, wasn't I?' to which the Duke, with rather more

34

tact than was his wont, would reply, 'I have often heard Your Highness say so'.

But, in fact, my concerns were slightly more peripheral; I was the desk officer in charge of the Council of Europe and Western European Union. As such I used to accompany the Parliamentary delegation to plenary sessions of the Assemblies of these two organisations in Strasbourg and in Paris. In that capacity I got to know a number of parliamentarians of all parties. It was there that I renewed acquaintance with Maurice Macmillan, whom I had known only slightly at Eton; and on the other side of the political divide I got to know and admire, if not always to respect, the mercurial George Brown.

I also occasionally accompanied the Minister to meetings of the Council of Europe or WEU Ministerial Council. The Minister was a newcomer to foreign affairs, a seemingly unqualified import from the Whips' Office and the Ministry of Labour, a Mr Edward Heath.

The Edward Heath that his parliamentary colleagues see is a very different animal from the Edward Heath that his civil servants see. It is true that his appetite for work was such that if he asked you to come and see him at 6 o'clock it was prudent to enquire whether that meant 6 am or 6 pm. But of the stiffness and shyness which make it so hard for MPs to relax with him, and such an ordeal to be stuck with him at a cocktail party, there was no trace. He was easy, relaxed, constantly pulling the legs of even quite junior officials and expecting to have his pulled in return.

Although I was not, as I have admitted, directly involved in the EEC negotiations, I was rubbing shoulders every day with those who were, and I saw a good many of the key policy documents. I saw at close quarters why Harold Macmillan was forced to the conclusion that Britain should seek membership of the Community, from which we had stood so aloof until then.

It may be as well to repeat the basic arguments as they appeared then; for they have lost none of their validity with the passage of thirty years; though the same sort of people, mostly on the left of the Labour Party and on the right of the Conservative Party, who rejected the arguments then, still astonishingly do so today.

The first argument is that, given Europe's repeated tendency to generate internal wars which spread with disastrous consequences for mankind, it must be to everyone's advantage, including ours, that the nations of Western Europe should pool their sovereignty in such a way as to deprive themselves of the practical means of going to war with one another. It is true that this particular argument does not require that Britain itself should be part of this integrated community; but it does mean that it is not acceptable for Britain to attempt to obstruct the process of integration, as Eden had attempted to do in 1955 with his Atlantic Community ideas, to which Gladwyn had been so strongly opposed. Churchill, who had never envisaged full British participation in an integrated Europe, nonetheless recognised the absolute need for the Continental countries to draw closer together, and for Britain to help, not hinder this process.

The second main argument was that Britain, as the industrialised nation most dependent on trade, needed to have sure, duty-free access to the market of 160 million consumers (now of course over 230 million) which was opening up on our doorstep, and from which it would be most damaging for British industry to be excluded. It followed, of course, that if Britain was to ensure unrestricted access to the European market, the Europeans would have to have unrestricted access to ours. It is relevant to point out that this argument holds good whether we are in a Common Market, or, as many of the opponents of the EEC say they would prefer, in a free-trade area instead.

But the really telling argument was the third one; and it is the one which is most often overlooked. Whether or not it is essential for Britain to be *in* the European Community, it is undoubtedly disastrous for us to be shut *out* of it. It is not so much that our goods would be shut out of Europe by the high walls of the Common External Tariff; far more serious would be the loss of our markets in third countries, including the countries of the Commonwealth, to products made within the EEC. The latter would be more competitive than anything we could produce because of the economies of scale which are possible in a guaranteed home market of nearly 200 million. The final, conclusive argument is that Britain must be able to influence developments on the Continent. With the advent of the European Community we can only do that from inside, and, Mrs Thatcher please note, from *right* inside.

It is extraordinary how these arguments have retained their validity despite the huge changes which have taken place during the past thirty years; and although they must be reassessed in the light of the amazing developments in Eastern Europe (I will attempt to do so later) their basic validity still holds good.

Nevertheless, however compelling the arguments for British membership of the EEC, they became purely academic when General de Gaulle vetoed the British application in 1962.

By that time I had left the Foreign Service. After four years in London, which I had much enjoyed, the time had come for another foreign posting. My wife and I looked at one another; did we really want to pull up our roots again, face leaving the children at home, perhaps thousands of miles away, or pulling them out of the schools where they were doing well and forcing them to start all over again? And where were we likely to be sent? The list of agreeable posts was discouragingly short; that of frankly unpleasant ones seemed interminable. No doubt a fortnight in Ouaga Dougou or Ulan Bator would be fun, but two years? And what lay at the end of the diplomatic road? Our Ambassador in Washington, Harold Caccia, was interviewed on the tarmac as he came home for his summer leave. 'What are you most looking forward to, Ambassador?' 'Having dinner alone with my wife; we haven't been able to do that for ten months.' What sort of a life is that? It may be worth it for the interest and excitement of Washington – but for Tegucigalpa?

In any case I was now so bitten by the idea of getting Britain into the EEC that I wanted to get more directly involved in the process (this was in July 1962, before de Gaulle's veto).

And so, in July 1962, I resigned from the Foreign Service after fifteen interesting and enjoyable years. I retain a great respect and admiration for the Service, which has served Britain well under governments of all political complexions. British interests are not best served when Prime Ministers such as Neville Chamberlain or Margaret Thatcher pander to the popular prejudice that the British Foreign Service is there to look after foreigners at the expense of Britain. On the contrary, it is the job of the Foreign Office to try to make British Ministers understand how their policies and actions are seen abroad, to help them to 'See ourselves as others see us', and to get used to being whipped, as the messenger bringing unpalatable news is whipped. It is sad to see the Foreign Office today being forced towards the kind of servile sycophancy endemic in the Soviet Foreign Service in pre-Gorbachev times.

And so, having been institutionalised for more than twenty years (four years in the Army and sixteen in the Civil and

Foreign Services), I was out in the world. I became the so-called Director of Research for the Common Market Campaign with a scruffy office well situated in Whitehall and no salary. In practice what I did was to go round the country speaking to captive audiences about the Common Market; and I found that public speaking was not alarming, but quite enjoyable. On behalf of the Common Market Campaign I attended the Conservative Party Conference at Llandudno in 1962. It was the last occasion on which the Tory Conference met in that most beguiling of resorts; it was also Harold Macmillan's last Conference, at which the old magician was on the very top of of his form before it all started to go so wrong. It was there, in scornful reference to Hugh Gaitskell's alleged dithering over Europe, that he gave his justly celebrated rendering of, 'She wouldn't say Yes, and she wouldn't say No'.

By the end of the summer I was being driven to the conclusion that, if I was serious about Britain joining the Common Market, I had better get involved with the party whose government was actually trying to do something about it; and so I joined the Conservative Party. It is as well to be absolutely frank about this, because it has been of great importance to me in the recent past, and it may well have even more importance in the future. I joined the Conservative Party because it was the party of Europe. Having joined it for that reason, I then found that I could accept most of its other policies. But I would not feel able to remain in a Conservative Party which reneged on its commitment to participation in Europe; all the more so since I feel increasing doubts about many of the other policies which the party has adopted in recent years.

It was Maurice Macmillan who inducted me into the Party; and at whose suggestion I went to South Battersea to learn the basic facts about work at the political grass roots. I was nominally the Treasurer of the South Battersea Conservative Association. The way I tell the story is that when I arrived as Treasurer the finances were in a parlous state; when I left, the Association was bankrupt. But whatever my shortcomings as a Treasurer, I certainly learned a lot about how a political party is run by voluntary effort. It was to stand me in good stead.

While I was still working for the Common Market Campaign I was asked by my friend Dr Alan Glyn, then MP for Clapham, if I could help him out by addressing a meeting in his constituency on the Common Market. This I did, in Clapham Public Baths. Alan was quite unreasonably impressed. So too was his agent, a diminutive, red-headed ball of fire called Madeline Morrison. Quite soon after this, Madeline left Clapham to take up the agent's job in Eton and Slough.

Having enlisted in the Conservative Party I now started thinking in terms of fighting a General Election on its behalf. I was already forty-three, so it was time to get moving. I put in applications for Dagenham, Lichfield and Tamworth, and Solihull. Quite rightly none of them would look at me.

Then I received a conspiratorial message from Alan Glyn. Would my wife and I come round to see him at his house in Cadogan Gardens at 11 the following night, and tell no-one that we were coming. There we found Alan, and Madeline Morrison.

Madeline had walked into a major crisis on her arrival in Eton and Slouth. It was a seat which had been very nearly won by Jack Page in 1959 (he missed it by only 88 votes). But now Jack Page had got himself elected for Harrow, and the local Association had picked the Conservative leader on the council as their new candidate. But he, poor man, had fallen foul of the tax laws, and was facing charges for which he was eventually convicted. The affair caused a scandal, and bitter divisions within the Conservative Association. Madeline needed a new candidate, and she needed one quickly. He had to be someone with no previous involvement in the affairs of the town; and she wanted one with plenty of time to give to nursing the constituency. In short she wanted me; all the more so since she knew that she would get my wife into the bargain, having seen us both at work in Battersea when she had been in Clapham.

Of course with my background of Eton, the Guards and the Diplomatic Service, and a title to make matters worse, I was not exactly the image that Slough, an essentially working-class town, was looking for. Did someone say, but surely it was *Eton* and Slough? It is as well to remember the legendary French recipe for Horse and Lark Pie, 'Take one horse and one lark'.

Eton, in fact, played an extremely small part in my life as MP. During the eighteen months that I was the Member I never received an official invitation to the school. The boys used to hang out of their windows and cheer as we drove past in our election Landrover, which was good for morale; and a few of the older ones came to lend a hand during the campaign. But canvassing Eton was an unrewarding experience; all the domestic staff seemed to be foreigners, most of the masters seemed to be socialists, and the boys were too young to vote. Only the retired college servants living in delightful back alleys of Eton High Street yielded any electoral dividends.

It was only after I had lost the seat that my wife and I received an invitation from the Headmaster, Anthony Chenevix-Trench, no great administrator but a teacher of genius and an extremely nice man, to be his guests for the 4th of June celebrations. We sat in great grandeur in the front row of rickety chairs on the grass of Fellow's Eyot to watch the procession of boats and the fireworks. Every so often one of the small boys sitting on the grassy bank in front of us would get up and climb over the diminutive Headmaster, saying, 'Frightfully sorry, I want to speak to my sister'. I could almost believe the apocryphal story of an earlier Headmaster, who was walking along the Eton pavement when he was pushed into the gutter by a very large boy. The Headmaster felt that some reproof was perhaps called for. So he said to the boy, 'Do you know who I am?' The boy replied, 'I haven't the foggiest idea'. 'I am the Headmaster.' 'Good God', said the boy, 'then you're a cousin of mine'.

Slough's concerns were rather more down to earth.

It might have been difficult even for Madeline Morrison to impose me on the rightly suspicious Tories of Eton and Slough had it not been for the Chairman, John Ward, now MP for Poole. John knew exactly how to handle the faction-riven group of voluntary workers who compose every Conservative Association; he used the right mixture of guile, charm and brutality, and it worked perfectly.

I do not think I am being immodest in claiming that the Tories of Eton and Slough had got quite a good bargain. As promised, they had got two for the price of one. And they had got two full-timers. For the next twelve months my wife and I canvassed every night from tea-time until after dark. By the end of that time we had called at pretty well every house in the constituency. We also attended every meeting of every organisation, voluntary or statutory, that we could insinuate ourselves into. Indeed, at the local Labour Party's annual dinner, the Chairman was unwise enough to claim that, 'This is the first function in Slough this year that the Conservative candidate hasn't attended'.

Slough had a large and steadily growing Asian population.

There was little racial tension, but it would be foolish to deny that there was some resentment among the indigenous white population; and this resentment tended to attach itself to the town's Labour MP, Fenner Brockway, whose sympathy with colonial peoples and whose crusades against race prejudice were well known. My wife and I went out of our way to get involved with the local Asian community; and I was scrupulous not to exploit the race issue against Fenner Brockway. But I have to admit that the end result was that quite a lot of the Asians voted for me because I had been nice to them, and had been able to attend more of their gatherings than the busy Fenner Brockway had been able to do, while all the racially prejudiced whites voted for me because at least I wasn't Fenner Brockway.

I certainly wasn't Fenner Brockway. I have been privileged to meet many great and noble men in my time; Fenner was the noblest, and one of the greatest. His kindness and generosity to me and my wife before, during and after the election campaign were endless; and I am glad to say that he remained a friend until the end of his life, and would invite us to all his major celebrations. I shared none of his views on economic matters; but I found myself agreeing with him, sometimes reluctantly, on many other matters such as race relations or the avoidance of conflict.

When we got to polling day on 15 October 1964 I knew that I had no real chance of winning. The polls were running steadily against the Conservatives; it was clear that the majority of 100 which had been won at the 1959 election was going to melt away, and that very many Conservative seats would be lost. There was no real prospect of actually winning a seat from Labour.

In the event, the Conservatives lost sixty-three seats. They won four, one of which was Eton and Slough. Over some of these four Conservative gains there hung a dark cloud; the suspicion, possibly not justified, that the Conservative candidate had exploited racial issues. No such suspicion hung over us in Eton and Slough.

It had been an astonishing day. My mother-in-law, aged 84, had broken her hip the night before, dashing to answer the telephone to get a message for us. My poor wife was distraught and would have rushed to her bedside, but was waved away with the order that her place was at her husband's side at this moment. From about 5 o'clock in the afternoon it rained steadily. By close of poll we were soaked to the skin, and certain that I had lost by a large margin. We retreated to a splendid Italian restaurant in Windsor to dry out and drown our sorrows. We arrived at the count in Slough's vast, barrack-like Community Centre, very convivial, nearly an hour after we have been told to get there. At the far end of the room Madeline Morrison was waving frantically. 'Where the hell have you been? I'm just about to demand a recount'.

We had three recounts. All but one gave me a majority; and in the end I was in by 11 votes. My mother-in-law, coming round after the anaesthetic, was told the result: 'You mean eleven thousand', she said and passed out again.

It was nearly two in the morning when the result was confirmed. My supporters were jubilant and carried me shoulder-high into the local party headquarters. All I felt was an immense sadness at having ended the Commons career of a man the latchet of whose shoe I was not worthy to unloose.

# CHAPTER FIVE

# The Wrong Sort
# of Tory

## 1964–1970

My career as MP for Eton and Slough was brief, and not particularly glorious, though it left me a few legacies which were to haunt me for years to come.

Having won the seat by a mere 11 votes, with another General Election clearly an early prospect, with Slough being a mere 15 miles from London, and my then home at Sunningdale a mere 5 miles from Slough, it was both natural and expected that I should continue to spend a great deal of my time nursing the constituency. On most days I visited Slough on my way up to London in the early morning, then on to the House of Commons for a morning's work; back to Slough for a lunch engagement, up to London in time for Questions; down to Slough for an early evening function, back to London for the 10 o'clock vote, and then sometimes even look in at the fag end of a function on my way home at 11 pm. Not a recipe for a quiet life – nor one for making a specially useful contribution to the work of the Commons.

Europe was no longer an issue at this time. De Gaulle had

slammed the door, seemingly for many years to come. But the issue of national sovereignty, which underlay much of the debate about the Common Market, did rear its head in another context; that of the independent nuclear deterrent. As a convinced believer in international co-operation and of multilateral defence, I deplored the Conservative stress on the absolute necessity of maintaining a purely British nuclear deterrent under our own sole control. Indeed, so distressed was I by the speech which Peter Thorneycroft, the Conservative spokesman on defence, made in the debate on the Queen's Speech that I very nearly committed the silly gesture of refusing to vote for my own party in the very first vote which I attended as an MP. I am sure that a lot of people will adduce this admission as evidence that I was never sound at any stage. If it makes them any happier I will freely admit that I have always had doubts about much Conservative policy, and still more doubts about many Conservative attitudes. But I still remain a Conservative supporter, I still continue to work for the Party; and it is only if the Party can attract and retain a large number of the sceptics that it can count on winning a majority.

But the independent deterrent, though a fertile subject for discussion, was not really a major political issue in the 1964–6 Parliament; after all, Labour was committed to keeping it. But there were three live issues, each of which was to have an influence on my future well after the end of that particular parliament.

The first was race relations, where I found myself more in sympathy with what the Labour Government was trying to do in their Race Relations Act than were most of my party.

The second was the abolition of capital punishment; the achievement of Sidney Silverman. Although I am, and have always been, an opponent of capital punishment, I have to confess that it is an issue on which I have on a couple of occasions shown cowardice or expediency. But in 1965 I voted firmly for abolition. Perhaps I should here explain my views on capital punishment, for they have never changed, even though I have not shown consistency in my votes on the issue.

I have always felt that the existence of capital punishment, even though it may deter some criminals (especially armed robbers) from killing, fosters a climate of violence in which the taking of life becomes less rather than more abhorrent. There is the morbid fascination, which would be whipped up by the tabloid press, surrounding the carrying out of the death penalty. I firmly believe that the mentally deranged, who constitute a high proportion of murderers anyway, are as likely to be drawn towards violent action by the possibility of ending on the scaffold as they are likely to be deterred. And, of course, the argument that the death penalty ought to be available for terrorist killers is the feeblest of all; terrorists have given proof time and time again that they are as ready to die as to kill for their warped beliefs. The only effect of executing them is to make them martyrs to their cause.

The third occasion for my stepping out of line was over oil sanctions against Rhodesia. The white minority in Rhodesia under Ian Smith's premiership had made a unilateral declaration of independence (UDI). This was clearly illegal, though Ian Smith had many unabashed sympathisers in the Conservative Party. After much dithering the Labour Government decided to comply with a United Nations call for oil sanctions against Rhodesia. The Conservative Party, still led by Alec Douglas Home, decided to abstain in the vote on the application of sanctions. A group of right-wingers, led by Julian Amery, decided to vote against the measure. Another group, mainly but not entirely left-wingers, decided to vote with the Labour Government in support of sanctions. I was one of them. A rather more distinguished 'rebel' was Sir Harry Legge Bourke, subsequently the Chairman of the 1922 Committee of Conservative backbenchers. Sir Harry was an old-fashioned honourable right-wing Tory, a breed now extinct. He took the view that Ian Smith was a traitor to Queen and Country, and should be treated accordingly.

My vote on Rhodesian sanctions caused me a good deal of trouble in the Slough Conservative Association; and much more trouble at a later stage in my career. Things were made worse by the right-wing MP, Patrick Wall, who came to my constituency and berated me to my women's branch as if I had voted against the Party (whereas in fact I had voted in favour of something on which the Party had abstained). I was saved, and taught a very useful lesson by Ted Leather, an ex-minister and subsequently Governor of the Bahamas who came to address a meeting. He expressed astonishment that anyone should dare to stand up for a cad like Smith who had let the Queen down, dammit; it was a jolly good show that their MP knew where his duty lay. I learned from this incident that, provided you get the rhetoric right, you can sometimes get people to swallow some unpalatable truths.

There is one small footnote to my undistinguished parliamentary career as MP for Slough 1964 to 1966. I was made a member of the Standing Committee which was carrying out a line-by-line examination of one of the Labour Government's Housing Bills. The leader on our side was John Boyd Carpenter, by far the most skilful debater I have ever listened to. He could get up at a moment's notice and give a detailed, convincing argument in favour of whatever course he was required to defend; an hour later he could, if required, argue the opposite case with equal clarity and conviction. I have heard only one other debater equally skilful, John Boyd Carpenter's star pupil, who owes him so much, Margaret Thatcher.

Alec Douglas Home, who had so unexpectedly succeeded Harold Macmillan as Prime Minister in 1963, had done extremely well to avert a Labour landslide in the October 1964 election. But he was not thought to be a match, as Leader of the Opposition, for Harold Wilson in the House of Commons. So the Tory Party decided that it wanted a new leader more in tune with the spirit of the age, and better able to parry Wilson's caustic wit. The choice lay between the brilliant, kindly, indolent Reggie Maudling and the more thrusting meritocratic Ted Heath. Ted won.

The irony was that on the very day that the election of a new leader was to be held, Alec having fairly readily agreed to step down, he himself found his form at the despatch box and, after one of Wilson's cheap but effective jibes, demolished him utterly with, 'I do wish that the Rt. Hon. Gentleman could sometimes remember that he is the Prime Minister'.

Ted Heath, as leader of the Party, made a flying visit to my supposedly marginal constituency during the 1966 election campaign. He arrived by helicopter at the edge of a crowded car-park meeting, which caused a stir. He then spoke for twenty minutes and sent everyone to sleep – until a blessed heckler piped up at the back and Ted crackled into top form, holding the crowd enthralled. Always see to it that you have a good heckler handy.

The 1966 election campaign was a chilly and miserable affair, of which I retain few happy memories. I still recall the feeling of bleak despair when I was spotted alone on a Council estate by a Labour car with a loudspeaker, knowing that the tide was running against me, and hearing the disembodied voice, 'Say goodbye to your Tory MP'. Canvassing is usually a surprisingly agreeable pursuit; people are astonishingly polite when you drag them from their favourite TV pro-gramme to their front door. This was one of the few cam-paigns where I had the door slammed in my face; and, at the very same moment I was stung by a wasp. Perhaps I might at this point tell my favourite canvassing story; though it actually happened to me during a later campaign, it shows the dangers of quick reactions. A man came across to me in a new, open-plan council estate. 'I'm 84', he said. I had just begun on 'You don't look a day older than 75', when he went on, 'Yes; me and 82 next door, we haven't had our grass cut for six weeks. What are you going to do about it?'

In March 1966 my career as MP for Slough came to a decisive end. I was out, not by 11 votes, but by 4,000 to a triumphalist Joan Lestor.

Being a MP, even so dim a one as I, is a full-time job, or at least it had been for me. When I lost, there was an awful feeling of emptiness. I had no job to go back to; once you leave the Foreign Service you cannot go back again. I waited in vain for offers of directorships. No one seemed to want me; indeed I did not have much to offer.

For some time I continued to nurse Eton and Slough, kidding myself that I might win it back one day. One incident I recall. There were one or two wards where it was exceedingly difficult to get a Conservative branch to function. One day Madeline Morrison came to me in great glee. 'I have managed to get a committee going in Farnham South. Come along to the inaugural meeting tonight'. When I came into the room I saw that all she had been able to do was to scrape together a few old work horses from neighbouring branches, and there were no new faces at all. Well, not strictly true. Sitting at the back were two dark-skinned gentlemen.

Now this was at a time when the nation, and very particularly the Conservative Party, was trembling at the prospect of a huge influx of Asians from Uganda, fleeing the savage persecution of Idi Amin; and, as with the Hong Kong Chinese, good Tories were demonstrating their ideological purity by denouncing the Government for flooding the country with immigrants.

Back to our branch meeting. As we progressed through the tedious agenda, we came to the bit where people were actually asked to *do* something. 'Who will go out and collect subscriptions?' Everyone stared into space; except two brown arms shot in the air. 'Who will deliver the leaflets?' Same gazing into space; same two brown arms in the air.

After the meeting I went up to the two volunteers. 'Where do you come from?' 'Uganda.' 'How long have you been in this country?' 'One week.' The first thing they had done on arrival had been to join the Conservative Party, which was indignantly demanding that the likes of them should be kept out.

It was not at that stage realistic to suppose that Slough could be won back; though won it was a few years later by John Watts. I needed to look for another seat; and in the meanwhile, something to fill my time. I offered my services, unpaid, to the Conservative Research Department, then still basking in the liberal, enquiring traditions of Rab Butler, and pleasantly housed in Old Queen Street. They found me something useful to do; to build bridges between the Party and the senior staff at the universities. It was a job which I enjoyed very much indeed, and which brought me into contact with some interesting people, among them a brilliant, rather wayward economist called Alan Walters. Moreover, the atmosphere in Research Department itself was congenial, with some of the Party's brightest young people working there; and frequent brain-storming meetings were held with Ted Heath, who had become Leader of the Party in 1965, Reggie Maudling, Enoch Powell, Rab Butler, and the wise Robert Fraser.

But my prime concern was to find myself another, winnable seat. Now my past began to catch up with me. I think I must hold some kind of record for the number of selection committees who turned me down. New Forest, Reigate, Hendon South, Chichester. At each of these I was beaten by a better candidate. But my vote in favour of Rhodesian sanctions, and for the abolition of capital punishment, told against me. Then, one day I was given a pretty clear signal in Research Department. Esher had been set up for me; I was to go flat out for it. And, indeed, I found the most friendly welcome at the Selection Committee, and at the subsequent meeting of the wider Executive Committee. I was now the hot favourite for adoption by a General Meeting of the whole Association. Two days before that meeting a piece appeared in the Cross Bencher column of the *Sunday Express*, at that time an influential voice on the far right of the Party. It ran somewhat as follows. 'The Tories of Esher are a good right-wing bunch. Why do they allow Conservative Central Office to foist on them a left-winger who is soft on immigration, hanging, and the defence of the white man in Africa? They should tell Sir Anthony Meyer to pack his bags and seek rich pickings somewhere else'.

As I entered that crowded room I could feel the hostility welling up from the floor. I didn't do at all well anyway, and was decisively rejected in favour of Carol Mather.

Failure breeds failure. I was now a reject; and was thrown out successively by Windsor and by Chertsey. Comic relief came in the form of an invitation to appear at South Fylde, for which I had not even sent my name in. After a very unsatisfactory interview with a small Selection Committee, I was told that I had won through to the semi-final. This was held in Kirkham Conservative Club, on what must surely have been the hottest March night ever recorded. There were seven semi-finalists. We were all ordered to be present at 7.30; and we drew lots. I drew the last slot; which meant a three-hour wait. By the time I got into the room the audience was past caring, and the smell of beer was overpowering. I made as bad a speech as I can ever recall making. Then came questions. 'What connection do you have with this area?' 'None', said I. Then, 'This, as you know, is an agricultural constituency. What do you know about agriculture?' 'Nothing', said I. There being no more questions I left the room. Five minutes later the Chairman came out. 'Very pleased to tell you that you are through to the final.' The final took place at Preston Town Hall. There were three of us. There were 800 in the hall; it was in fact the first of the 'primaries'. For once I spoke really well. I came bottom; but between me, who came bottom, and Edward Gardner, who came top, there were only seven votes difference, out of 800.

I seemed to be getting nowhere fast. And, after eighteen months of quite busy unpaid work in Research Department I began to feel that I was worth as much to them as they were paying me. My feelings came to the boil after I had located a very bright professor of urban studies, Professor Parry Lewis, in Manchester University who was working on a scheme for revitalising run-down city areas by judicious use of small subsidies and tax incentives so as to smarten up the corner shop and the pub, tidy up the railings and the grass, sweep the streets more often, and induce more people to come and live in the area. This, at a time when such areas were being bulldozed and planted with tower blocks, seemed to me an eminently practical approach, and one which accorded well with Conservative philosophy. The professor wanted to employ a research assistant to help him prepare a study on this theme, and a guarantee of eventual publication. I asked the Party Treasurer for £1,500 to cover the research assistant for a year and the cost of publication. After much thought, and considerable delay, the answer came back that the Party could not afford this expenditure. So I decided that if they could not afford that they could not afford my zero salary either; and I left.

While I was working in Research Department there was a lively debate going on about the future of economic policy, in view of the now palpable failure of the Labour Government to find a way of controlling the slowly rising level of inflation. The idea gained ground that the most effective, and the least politically painful, way of controlling inflation was by strict control of the money supply; and it was this doctrine which was adopted at a famous, indeed now notorious weekend meeting of the Shadow Cabinet at Selsdon Park. It seems that the doctrine was enthusiastically embraced by all those present, including Iain Macleod, the Shadow Chancellor, with just one exception – Peter Walker – who regarded it as far too simplistic, and who found it inconsistent with his view of the obligation of the state to play an active role in stimulating the economy by judicious intervention when and where necessary.

I was insufficiently sure of myself in economic matters to venture any criticism of the new craze for monetarism; indeed, as far as I can recall I went along with it quite happily. Moreover, concerned as I still was to find myself a seat, and burdened as I was with a left-wing reputation it was a godsend to find one issue on which I could agree wholeheartedly with the right.

It seemed to me that I could do both myself and the Party some good if I could find a way of putting across these right-wing economic ideas in conjunction with rather more liberal ideas on social matters. There did not seem to be any publication offering this kind of combination. Why should I not publish just such a periodical myself?

I knew nothing at all about magazine production, so I sought advice. My place as candidate at Eton and Slough had been taken by Nigel Lawson, then editor of the *Spectator*. I had given him some help when he took over from me; and presuming on that, and on our previous acquaintance, I went to seek his advice. He said, 'What you want is an editor. Why don't you go and see T. E. (Peter) Utley?' Utley was the legendary, blind leader-writer on the *Telegraph*, who sadly died recently. I had heard him speak, and was dazzled by his brilliance; and in particular by his argument that the abolition of the death penalty, because it ran counter to the strong feelings of the British people, had done damage to the man in the street's faith in Parliament, and that any gain from abolition was far outweighed by the harm which it did to the cause of parliamentary democracy.

It was I who chose the rather pretentious title of the magazine, *Solon*, after the stern but wise law-giver of ancient Athens. I wanted to convey a slightly detached, academic flavour; and anyway it looked good set up on our masthead. It was Utley who defined the basic purpose of the magazine, to 'civilise the backlash'.

Utley and I worked very happily together on the first three numbers of this quarterly publication. I paid him a fee for each number, and I paid the £50 fee for each contributor, many of whom were well-known Fleet Street names suggested by Utley.

We had quite a distinguished list of contributors; in our first number a prescient piece by Lord Eccles on One World Toryism, which makes today's Little Britain Toryism look very lilliputian, and poems by Lord Hailsham and Enoch Powell. In a later number Nicholas Ridley made a passionate plea for a fully integrated European Community including Britain; Norman Gash defended Peel as a statesman who could rise above purely party loyalty; and John Barnes eloquently defended Stanley Baldwin, the great reconciler. Peter

Utley, who was himself involved in the Northern Irish scene, devoted most of the third issue to articles in support of the moderate Unionist stance.

However, the magazine never looked like covering its costs of production. I consulted a fellow called John Selwyn Gummer who was in the magazine world. It became clear that if I put in another £5,000 of my own money I could get the magazine to cover its costs; but it would never pay its way or recover my £5,000 for me. So, sadly, I had to shut it down. I did the last number myself, without Peter Utley's help, but that was the end.

Meanwhile, my quest for a seat seemed to have ground to a halt. My wife and I, with my mother-in-law and our youngest daughter, were holidaying in Ireland. At the hotel in Sligo there was a message from my son, back in London. 'Central Office has rung up. Would you let your name go in for West Flint?' 'I don't think I would be much good for a Scottish seat', said I. 'It's not Scotland, it's Wales'.

The sitting MP for West Flint was Nigel Birch, the man who had precipitated Harold Macmillan's departure by quoting Browning's Lost Leader, 'Never glad confident morning again', and who earlier had led the mass walk-out of Macmillan's entire team of Treasury ministers in protest against Macmillan's 'inflationary' public expenditure plans.

I went to see Nigel Birch, whom I had known very slightly as a colleague in 1964–6. To my astonishment he was not merely friendly, but eager to help. Why? The answer is a bit long, but it is a good story.

While I was in the middle of my fruitless seat-hunting I was rung up one day by Maurice Macmillan. 'I was thinking what I could do to help. I have arranged for you to speak to the Conservative Party's Finance Committee the week after next, on banking and the Common Market. You may meet some useful allies there.' 'But Maurice', I protested feebly, 'I have never been inside a bank except to cash a cheque'. 'Good Lord; I thought you were a merchant banker. Well, it's too late now. The meeting has been notified on the Whip'.

I spent the next ten days in frantic pursuit of knowledge, ruthlessly wining and dining any banker with whom I could scrape an acquaintance. On the dreaded day I turned up at room 14, the huge committee room where the Finance Committee meets on a Tuesday afternoon. There were five bored-looking members present, and Nigel Birch in the chair. 'We are very honoured today,' he said, 'to have Sir Anthony Meyer. Probably no one living knows more about banking and the Common Market than he does'. He then sat down, and went fast asleep, which was the wisest thing to do.

I then delivered myself of the drivel which I had prepared, for some ten minutes, praying that the earth would open and swallow me. But rescue was at hand. One of the five members present was Sir Alex Spearman. Now when I had been in the Embassy in Paris ten years earlier, Alex Spearman used to make a habit of breaking his journey home from the Côte d'Azur in Paris, and of coming to see me to be filled in on current developments in the French political scene. So, having listened to my burbling for ten minutes, he led the questioning. 'That was very interesting in its way. But what I would really like to hear from you is your assessment of General de Gaulle's chances of being able to carry through the decolonisation of Algeria.'

For twenty minutes I answered questions on this with such assurance that there was much banging on desks (which is how MPs indicate approval), creating enough noise to waken Nigel Birch, who was forever afterwards convinced that I was some kind of financial expert.

At any rate he had decided that I was the chap he wanted

to succeed him. His prime concern was to prevent the seat going to one particular local candidate whom he regarded as dangerously unstable. The only other possible local candidate was the Association Chairman, Michael McEvoy, but he had no wish to be an MP (nor had he thirteen years later, when I pressed him to take on the job). Birch was convinced that no local candidate other than McEvoy could prevent the seat from falling into undesirable hands; he therefore needed to bring in a candidate from outside; and, for the strange reasons I have just explained, he decided that I was the man to do it.

So it was that everything was made easy for me; and although I did not perform particularly well at any of the interviews, I won the nomination from the far more capable Ian Gow and Michael Howard. Ten months later I was the MP for West Flint, a seat I have not even heard of eighteen months earlier.

# CHAPTER SIX

# The Breakdown of Consensus

## 1970–1979

The 1970 election was the one which Edward Heath won despite all the predictions of the pollsters. I was going to Westminster to sit on the Government side of the House.

I made it very plain at the election count that it was my ambition to be a good constituency member; and that I had neither expectation nor desire for office of any kind. I was, however, faced immediately with a request from Maurice Macmillan, who had been appointed Chief Secretary to the Treasury, to be his Parliamentary Private Secretary (PPS, who is not paid for the job, is his Minister's eyes and ears in the Commons, and his channel of communication with backbench members). I had no desire for even this humble job, but I accepted it out of friendship for Maurice, and I followed him when he moved from the Treasury to the more stormy waters of the Department of Employment in the middle of a rail strike. There was another PPS in that Department at that time, Norman Tebbit. I have always found him a stimulating and congenial man; but the right-wing views which he expresses in public are very palid compared to those he airs in private. Maurice's Press Officer at the Department of Employment was a tough, genial but unscrupulous Yorkshireman called Bernard Ingham; I remember thinking that he was the sort of chap I would rather have on my side than against me.

Mr Heath's Government of 1970–4 spent very little of its time in calm waters. The major achievement was, of course, the successful conclusion of the negotiations for Britain's entry into the EEC; an achievement made possible by Mr Heath's visionary persistence, but also by the replacement of General de Gaulle by the more flexible but equally able President Pompidou. One offshoot of the burgeoning relationship between Mr Heath and President Pompidou was the setting up of the Franco-British Council, a semi-governmental organisation designed to stimulate contacts at every level between the British and the French people in the same way that contacts between French and West Germans had been stimulated through the close working relationship of de Gaulle and Adenauer. The Franco-British Council is still doing a useful job today, and I am proud to be the Deputy Chairman of the British section of the joint Council.

Entry into the EEC brought the European issue back to the centre of the political stage, the more especially so since a divided Labour Party decided to make the maximum political capital out of the traditional and natural reluctance of the British people to get too closely involved with overseas people who spoke foreign languages. I was appalled to see a party which preached the brotherhood of man pandering so crudely and so cynically to the nastiest kind of xenophobia; all the more so since their leaders knew perfectly well that Britain had no choice but to join the EEC, and, when they came to power themselves, were forced to act accordingly. Even more dismaying was to see lifelong supporters of the EEC like Roy

Hattersley paddle tamely in Harold Wilson's scummy wake, and vote against the Second Reading of the European Communities Bill for fear of losing their jobs. All the more credit to that tiny band of Labour MPs who that day stood up to be counted; the only survivor today is Tam Dalyell, and I take this opportunity to salute a kindred spirit.

But the Heath Government's existence was dominated by the battle to withstand the power of the trade unions, in the context of the parallel battle to contain inflation.

Ever since Churchill had given his Minister of Labour, Walter Monkton, a free hand in 1952 to settle with the unions at whatever price was necessary to avoid industrial conflict, successive governments had steadily retreated before the encroachments of trade union power. I am not making any value judgement, nor seeking to brand union leaders, even the most militant of them, as 'the enemy within'. It is the job of a union leader to get as much money for his members as he can; and if he fails to do so he will lose members to a rival union which can demonstrate more industrial muscle. In a situation of nil unemployment, which prevailed until the mid-1970s, the power of the unions to extort pay rises from employers, whether in the public or the private sector, was huge. The only surprising thing was how long this malign process took to produce its inevitable inflationary consequence.

In 1968 Harold Wilson accepted that he had to do something to check the unopposed growth, and hence mounting abuse, of trade union power. Barbara Castle, Minister of Labour, was authorised to produce proposals, based on the work of Lord Donovan's Royal Commission (a useful but now extinct species), for setting a framework of law for industrial relations. She produced a document called *In Place of Strife*. These proposals came to nothing, because of the implacable refusal of the trade unions, who were still, after all, Labour's paymasters, to have anything to do with them; and because of the connivance by some members of Harold Wilson's Government in the trade union campaign of non-compliance. Prominent among these defectors was James Callaghan. Among the few who stood by Harold Wilson to the end was George Thomas; and since I have some words of criticism about him a little later, I am glad to pay tribute to his staunchness on this occasion.

When the Heath Government came to power in 1970 it grasped this nettle firmly, but with fatal clumsiness. What it should have done was to pick up Barbara Castle's scheme exactly as it stood, which would have crippled any Labour attack. Instead it put together a team of lawyers to produce a mighty great bible covering in the greatest detail every aspect of industrial relations. The House of Commons sat through most of 1971 struggling night after sleepless night with this hydra. It proved totally unenforceable; and Labour repealed it as their first act on returning to power in 1974. This is one of the areas where Mrs Thatcher showed herself more skilful and more supple than Mr Heath.

Against this background of a steadily failing attempt to curb trade union power by legislation, the Heath Government was trying to master the sinister rise in inflation; and attempting to do so without allowing the equally alarming rise in unemployment to get out of hand. It will be recalled that Heath had come to power as the very model of a modern monetarist; with the most commendable determination to let industry fend for itself.

But unemployment was creeping up; and most alarmingly so in Scotland. The Upper Clyde Shipyard, having priced itself out of world markets by antiquated working practices, excessive wage rises and low productivity, was threatened with closure. Thousands of jobs were at risk in Glasgow where unemployment was already uncomfortably high.

It was the famous 'U-Turn'. Out of the window went all the clever notions so gleefully adopted at Selsdon Park three years earlier. Interventionism was back in a big way.

Once the Government was back in the business of helping lame ducks over stiles, it was forced back into the business of controlling wages and prices. And Maurice Macmillan, now back in the Treasury as Paymaster General, was in charge of the Government's Counter Inflation Bill; and as his PPS I was behind him when he confronted as best he could the mocking hostility of Conservative MPs like Nigel Lawson, John Biffen, John Nott and Nicholas Ridley, who had retained their faith in the God of Selsdon Park.

I have never concealed my admiration for Mr Heath, who has breadth of vision and a generosity of spirit of which Mrs Thatcher is quite incapable. His defects are all too apparent; and none more than his obsessional resentment of Mrs Thatcher's treatment of him after her election victory in 1979, when she pointedly refused to include him in her Government or to give him a post commensurate with his gifts.

He had his shortcomings also as a party leader. I have spoken earlier of his easy relations with his civil servants. To that I might add that he is one of the wittiest and most agreeable after-dinner speakers I have ever heard. But he finds it very hard to chat to MPs. He rarely came into the Smoke Room or the Dining Room, and never into the more informal Tea Room. There is a story of his then PPS saying to him, 'Ted, you really must make an effort to be nice to some of the chaps. Why don't you go and have a drink in the Smoke Room one day?' Two days later the PPS was delighted to see Ted in the Smoke Room, chatting to a very senior back-bencher. The PPS crept up behind, just in time to hear Ted say, 'That was a bloody awful speech you made in the debate yesterday'. He was indeed his own worst enemy.

I spent the next thirteen years getting to know and love my West Flint constituency, about which I had been so shamefully ignorant at the outset. Of course there were occasions when I found myself athwart my more orthodox party workers, and there was one major issue where I found myself having to do battle with my own Government, over the proposal to close down the Shotton steelworks on the edge of my constituency. I felt it right to join forces with the Labour MP in whose constituency Shotton was situated in his gallant fight to resist the closure.

One small incident which occurred during these years is of sufficient relevance to my main theme to be worth recalling here. One of the factors in the victory which I had won in 1964 in Slough had been the massive help which I received from Conservatives in the neighbouring constituency of South Bucks. The MP was the highly unorthodox extreme right-winger, Ronald Bell. There was hardly a single issue on which I agreed with him, except that he too was opposed to capital punishment; but I got on well with him, and was grateful for his help. In 1973 a group of his party workers, on the instigation of one of them who wanted the seat himself, made a move to get Ronald Bell deselected. It seemed to me quite unacceptable to deselect a hard-working and very effective MP merely because his views were unfashionable at that time; and I wrote a strongly worded letter to *The Daily Telegraph* to support Bell, and to deplore the attempt to deselect him. I have some reason to suppose that this letter played a part in defeating the move. It also, incidentally, spoilt the chances of Michael Heseltine, whose own Devon seat had been redistributed out of existence and who would have stood a much better chance of inheriting Bell's seat than any of the plotters against him.

As 1973 wore on the skies began to darken. Mr Heath's new policy of co-operation between unions, management and government, the policy castigated as corporatism by the true monetarists, was coming unstuck. It was coming unstuck because moderate trade union leaders could not keep their side of any bargain struck with the Government; they were forever being outbid by their own extremists. The crunch came when Joe Gormley, the miners' leader, was unable to get his union executive to accept a pay package which he had negotiated with the Coal Board, and which he had promised the Government he would easily be able to sell to his own people.

As the coal strike slipped steadily out of the hands of moderate leaders, it became clear that what was now at issue was how far the writ of the elected government ran. That was the question which Mr Heath put squarely to the British people at the ill-timed February 1974 election. The British people were asked whether they wanted to be ruled by an elected government, or by the union bosses, frequently elected for life on a most dubious suffrage. The British people gave their answer, loud and clear. It was, 'We couldn't care less'.

And so in 1974, Labour scraped in; and again, with a very slightly larger majority, in October that year. As far as economic policy goes, they governed by kind consent of the TUC, to which all awkward questions were referred. The first act of the incoming Labour Government was to repeal Mr Heath's ill-fated Industrial Relations Act. Needless to say, they made no attempt to revive the notions which they had subscribed to six years earlier in 'In Place of Strife'.

These were depressing, worrying days. The devotion of the British people to democracy seemed painfully fragile. Any extremist with a talent for swaying crowds could have posed a real threat to our system of parliamentary government. There were some of us, drawn from all parties, and from all wings of those parties, who believed that the only way to restore the authority of elected government was to get together a government of national unity, under some widely acceptable figure such as Roy Jenkins, to bring the unions back within the rule of law, to maintain a barrier against price and incomes rises in the public and in the private sectors, and to give a major boost to industrial investment over current consumption. In an article which I wrote in May 1974, I expressed these anxieties, and these hopes.

> Everything that has happened since the General Election shows that our present two party system cannot sustain the policies which are essential to prevent Britain from sliding downhill with gathering speed.
>
> The first task, and the one which commands all others, is to restore the authority of democratically elected government and the unchallenged rule of law. After the succession of setbacks which have taken place since the 'In Place of Strife' episode in 1969, and now the triumph of rebellion in Northern Ireland, it is not going to be possible for any government fully to assert its authority unless it can rely on the support of the official opposition. But it is the normal role of an opposition to bring discontented groups into alliance against the government.
>
> Only a powerful and widely supported government can ride out the latest wave of inflation – inexorably rising prices with stagnant production. It is not just a question of enforcing equality of sacrifice. It is also necessary deliberately to lower people's expectations. But

the role of an opposition is to arouse expectations that it could offer more if it were in office.

If Britain's present decline is not to become permanent and irreversible our already diminishing living standards must be still further depressed in order to release resources for capital investment. But it requires a very strong government to prevent a hungry populace from raiding the stocks of seed corn, especially if the opposition is accusing the government of deliberately starving the masses for ideological purposes.

As Britain's plight deteriorates the two party system, which seemed so fragile on the morrow of the indecisive election, seems rather to solidify and to make it that much harder to break out of the vicious circle. And yet there is an astonishingly wide measure of consensus stretching across all the parties as to what needs to be done. If it were not for the obstacles presented by the two party system it would be possible to find a substantial majority to support a short term emergency programme based on:

1. The restoration of the authority of government, with the Trade Unions and other powerful minorities occupying a key place which they themselves would have had a hand in defining.

2. An incomes policy which will limit wage-initiated inflation and do something to alleviate the social injustices which are inevitable when the economy is contracting.

3. The need to set aside sufficient resources for investment, to reward scarce skills, and to provide some incentive for the wealth creators despite growing popular demands for more equality and more current consumption.

4. The absolute need to maintain continuity in foreign and defence policy.

It would not be difficult to work out a detailed programme of action for the next two years or so based on these four points which would be acceptable to a very large number of MPs in all parties.

This is not to argue for a formal coalition. The Labour Party's opposition to a peace time coalition is almost insuperable because of the memories of 1931. Things will have to get much worse before this psychological barrier can be breached. By then events may be moving too fast to rescue anything in the centre.

So can nothing be done at this stage? Might it not be a stabilising factor if a sizeable group of Members, of all parties, were to come together in order to agree, first privately, and then, at the appropriate moment publicly on a broad programme such as that described, and to commit themselves to support these measures if they were carried out by the government – regardless of what government it was? This would provide a broadly based centre at a critical time, and lessen the danger that, as in Northern Ireland, a frightened populace would seek security at the political extremes.

To judge by their public utterances there were many prominent figures in all three parties who would have been ready to put aside their ideological prejudices long enough to get such a programme moving. The idea attracted predictable ridicule from the ideological purists on both sides of the party divide; and, in the event, hardly any of those who supported the idea were prepared to stand up and be counted when the grapeshot started to whistle around. I still believe that if it had been possible to form such a government and to carry through such a programme, Britain could have been saved much suffering, and we could, after an interlude, have returned to our party political games in a happier frame of mind.

Although quite a number of Conservative and Liberal MPs showed active interest in the idea, there was little or no response from anyone in the Labour Party. In any case, Labour's second electoral victory, in October 1974, though it left them with a majority which proved insufficient to withstand a series of by-election defeats, nonetheless rendered ideas of a coalition government somewhat academic.

I doubt whether even the Labour Party will be tempted to claim 1974–9 as their golden years. They were years of mounting inflation, rising unemployment, falling production, and humiliating recourse to the IMF. Eventually a government which had resolved to be resolute in all its dealings with the unions was destroyed by the backlash from a strike in the lower paid echelons of the Health Service; even abject surrender to the unions did not buy industrial peace.

One particularly inglorious episode from that period has left me with a permanent contempt for the Labour Party. In 1977 there was a prolonged and very bitter strike by the firemen. A group of five firemen at Rhyl in my constituency refused to take part in industrial action which could have threatened lives; and insisted on carrying on working. I was not surprised by the bullying tactics used by the Fire Brigades Union to isolate, almost to intimidate, these five men. But I was shocked at the attitude of some senior fire officers who found it embarrassing that some of the men under their command should dare to make a stand in this way; and I was horrified by the refusal of the Labour Home Secretary, that profoundly decent and honourable man, Merlyn Rees, to give any kind of public encouragement to men who were putting their duty to the public above the pressures being exerted on them by the union. This episode reinforced me in my belief that, for all their fine talk, no Labour Government will ever dare to face out the unions.

There were two issues in that 1974–9 Parliament which are of relevance to my story. The first was the 1975 EEC Referendum, the dodgy device which Harold Wilson used to get himself off the hook (as he might more wittily have put it, 'he had nailed his trousers to the mast, and now wanted to get down'); for he had inveighed so powerfully against the EEC that it was now awkward for him to admit that he had no choice but to stay put in it. There was a national referendum campaign, and I found myself campaigning alongside supporters of the EEC in all parties, both nationally and in and around my constituency.

It was a wonderful feeling to be campaigning for a cause in which I believed with no reservation, and alongside people with whom I had so much, apart from party labels, in common.

The second was the debate on the Labour Government's proposals for a measure of devolution for Scotland and Wales. Before the 1970 election the Conservatives under Mr Heath, and more especially under the influence of Sir Alec Douglas Home, had accepted the idea of an elected Scottish Assembly, though the idea was never translated into draft legislation in the 1970–4 Parliament. Under Mrs Thatcher's leadership the party did an about turn, and any idea of devolution was dropped. When Labour brought forward their very ill-considered scheme, which would have created elected assemblies with power to spend money but no responsibility for raising it, the Conservative Party had little hesitation in opposing it. But the debates which followed, and which took up the greater part of the 1976–7 parliamentary session, were the finest debates it has ever been my privilege to listen to.

The Conservatives were pretty well united in their opposition to the schemes, and there were some effective attacking speeches; though there remained some, notably Alick Buchanan Smith, who remained faithful to the ideas of Heath and Douglas Home for an elected Scottish Assembly; Alick himself was dismissed by Mrs Thatcher for his stand on this.

But for most of us the fascination was in the eloquent and passionate unpredictability of the contributions from the labour side. There was Eric Heffer, sounding like a resurrected G. K. Chesterton, speaking of the people of England who would not let their country be split asunder; Tam Dalyell, on his feet night after night pointing out the unacceptability of Scottish MPs legislating for England while English MPs would be debarred from legislating for Scotland (this argument became famous as the 'West Lothian Question' after the name of Tam's constituency); and a succession of speeches at once lucid and passionate from the greatest parliamentary orator of our time, the late, deeply lamented John Mackintosh, the only one of this group who supported devolution.

I spoke on platforms throughout Wales against Devolution, and took part in the referendum campaign in Wales, which rejected it overwhelmingly. I found myself alongside some strange allies, but none stranger than Neil Kinnock.

I have no regrets at having played my tiny part in sinking the Welsh part of the scheme; though even at the time I felt a little queasy at the manner in which the people of Scotland were deprived of their Assembly, because the votes in favour just failed to attain the qualified majority which had been inserted into the Bill by the procedural skill of Labour's George Cunningham. The proposals were ill thought out, and, in the case of Wales at least, untimely.

I am not sure that I would be equally ready today to go along with Conservative opposition to any more coherent schemes of devolution for Scotland and Wales. If the Conservatives win the next General Election, and that is still entirely possible, it is likely that they will do so solely on the strength of a majority of seats in England. There is a very real possibility that they could be left with not more than two seats in Scotland and not many more in Wales. In that case I do not see how they could credibly claim to be an acceptable government for the United Kingdom; indeed the strains which would be put on the unity of the kingdom from widespread refusal of the Scots and the Welsh to accept the democratic validity of such a government could not, in my opinion, be successfully withstood. In those circumstances I believe that the only way out would be to accord a large measure of autonomy to Scotland and to Wales. An elected Assembly would be but the first and most immediate concession that would need to be offered. The eventual solution would have to be a fully federal structure for the UK with a large degree of self-government for Scotland and for Wales, and wide-ranging devolution of responsibilities to the English regions.

# CHAPTER SEVEN

# The Advent of Mrs Thatcher

## 1979–1981

In 1975 Margaret Thatcher, invoking the machinery provided in 1965 for the annual election of the Party leader, had put her name into ballot against Mr Edward Heath; and after a brilliantly master-minded campaign by Airey Neave, defeated him. Shortly thereafter she came on a visit to North Wales and to my constituency in particular. I had made no secret of having voted against her in the leadership contest. I have to admit that I found her brand of Conservatism unsympathetic; though it was impossible, even then, to withhold admiration for her fantastic determination and energy.

Only once before had someone with so little experience and so few qualifications taken over the job of a Conservative leader – Bonar Law; Stanley Baldwin had, at least, been in the Treasury as Financial Secretary, and had a depth of experience of government at many levels. Mrs Thatcher had been a controversial Education Secretary; and was known to the public primarily for her (perfectly sensible) decision to spend money on education rather than on free milk. But she became known as

Maggie Thatcher, the Milk Snatcher, and the term of abuse contained just enough of a germ of truth to stick. Her toughness and her doctrinaire attitudes were already apparent; she was often described as the best man in the Cabinet. I remember taking a young student teacher up to her at this time. Mrs Thatcher gave the student her entire attention. However, it soon became clear that, although she was listening, she was taking no notice of what the young girl was saying; she was simply waiting to read her a (very pertinent) lecture on personal responsibility.

What I found particularly alarming during her visit was her habit of shooting from the hip. She made a number of speeches, many of them covering specific issues of policy; but she had prepared no press releases, so the world was dependent on the not very highly developed shorthand talent of our local reporters. I recall in particular a meeting of the National Federation of the Self Employed at Prestatyn at which, at the conclusion of a lengthy meeting, a questioner from the back asked her what changes she was going to make in the Party's policy for prices and incomes (a policy to which the Heath Government had been driven by harsh necessity in 1973, and which was being applied with diminishing success by the Labour Government). Mrs Thatcher's reply had the merit of brevity. 'We shall have *no* prices or incomes policy.' It was the first that anyone had heard of so fundamental a change in the Party's economic strategy; and it came, not as part of a prepared speech, but as an impromptu reply to an unforeseeable question. It is hard to think of a clearer, or a more dismaying example of what is meant by shooting from the hip; and I was appalled. But the very next day I was overcome with admiration by the way she moved in on Mold street market, taking over stalls, shouting their wares, and selling off

74

most of the contents in record time to the huge delight of stall-holders and general public alike.

I had, as I have said, my misgivings over Mrs Thatcher's style and, more fundamentally, over her vision of Britain. I think it would be fair to say that Mrs Thatcher's election victory in 1979 was due much more to the manifest disintegration of the Labour Government in the face of trade union militancy than to her own very real merits or the more dubious attractions of the policies which she offered.

I expressed these concerns in an article which I wrote in October 1981; in which, incidentally, I picked out Michael Heseltine as a future leader of the kind of Tory Party I would be proud to belong to. It was entitled 'There must be Hope too'.

The *Sunday Express* of October 18th carries a cartoon by Cummings (whose style of caricature is queasily reminiscent of the anti-semitic cartoons in the Nazi *Der Sturmer*) showing Mrs Thatcher staggering under the burden of a huge rock labelled 'The Legacy of the Ghastly Mistakes of Callaghan, Heath, Wilson, Jenkins, Macmillan, The Trade Unions and Management'. Surely there is one name missing from this catalogue of 'guilty men'; that of Winston Churchill. For it was Churchill, who, coming back into power in 1951, appointed Sir Walter Monckton as Minister of Labour with the express instruction that he was to establish and maintain good relations with the Trade Unions.

Now it may well be that Mrs Thatcher is doing everything right, and all her predecessors, Conservative as well as Labour, did everything wrong. It just seems to me a funny way of going about things for a Conservative Prime Minister, or rather, her over-zealous propagandists, to denigrate all the work of previous governments, and in particular that of Mr Heath's Government which took so many of the difficult decisions, not always correctly, but certainly decisively.

Not only is there denigration by some of Mrs Thatcher's propagandists of the record of all previous governments; there is also rejection by them of whole sections of the nation. This was all too evident in the unpleasant debate on Law and Order which took place on the first day of the Tory Party Conference at Blackpool, in which the fair-minded and warm-hearted Willie Whitelaw, to whom the Tory Party owes a huge debt for his steadfast loyalty, was repeatedly heckled, and the Conference threw out an inoffensive resolution on the grounds that it was not tough enough. There are some in the Conservative Party who would have us turn our backs on the dispossessed of our inner cities and of the third world, and who are in no way disconcerted that the party is losing so much sympathy among the ethnic minorities, among the young and, indeed, among the churches. It is perhaps significant that so many of these complacent Conservatives describe themselves as Whigs, not Tories. I have little doubt that they would have fought against Lord Shaftesbury's Factory Acts, on the grounds that child labour was an efficient way of creating the wealth from which the whole nation would benefit.

Despite these misgivings I still believe that Mrs Thatcher is doing what has to be done, and that she should be supported in doing it. Britain has to earn its living in a world which is not a 'compassionate society'. We cannot spend more than we earn. We have been doing it for some time, and financing it largely out of the

North Sea oil – and that, incidentally, is the answer to
those who ask 'Where has the North Sea oil money gone
to?' Indeed we have got to spend a great deal less than
we earn, so as to save the money to provide the three
million extra jobs we need. And that means that
everyone has got to accept a cut in their living standards.
Mrs Thatcher and Sir Geoffrey Howe have been the first
statesmen with the courage and honesty to say this out
loud. All honour to them. But if she is to carry the nation
with her, Mrs Thatcher must see to it that the sacrifices
are fairly spread. It is not acceptable that widows with a
tiny pittance on top of the state pension should have to
pay income tax while Ministers still talk about their aim
to cut the standard rate of tax on husbands and wives
who are both in well paid jobs.

And then Mrs Thatcher must offer hope. We know
that the tunnel is long and dark; but the light at the end
of it must illuminate some message more inspiring than
'Single Figure Inflation' or even 'Lower Interest Rates'.
We must be offered the vision of a society where a
fraction of even the present industrial work force, on a
shorter working week and longer holidays and a shorter
working life, nonetheless produces enough wealth to
finance lavish social services and a truly civilised
environment. I know that we cannot afford even the
present totally inadequate social services. But it is just
not true that they are overmanned. There are not enough
teachers or welfare workers or nurses. There are more
than we can afford, but that is quite another story; and
the Conservative Government should take a lot more
care than it is doing not to get the two stories muddled
up.

With unmatched courage and determination Mrs

Thatcher is leading the nation in the right direction. That is one half of what is meant by leadership. But she will not succeed unless she gets the nation to follow. To do that she must offer hope, and she must offer reconciliation. That does not mean compromise. It means accepting that the sudden emergence of differing views at the Blackpool Conference shows that there are other ways of reaching the objective which all Conservatives share; and that all those other ways have one thing in common; the need to return to the idea of One Nation. Mrs Thatcher might begin by paying less attention to her toadies on the *Express* and *Telegraph*, the Monday Club and the Selsdon Group. It was a pity she was not in the hall to hear Michael Heseltine. He is, after all, the Minister who has been most successful in achieving her aim of cutting public expenditure. But it is upon him that the mantle of the late, great Ian Macleod has clearly fallen. Nor did he waste the time he spent in Liverpool. To a Conference which had earlier rejected the decencies of Willie Whitelaw, and which was to cheer Norman Tebbit, when he dismissed the problems of Liverpool by saying it had only itself to blame, Heseltine spoke of the young black Britons (not immigrants), and the despairing young whites of the inner cities, and the moral impossibility of solving our problems by sweeping them aside; he was cheered when he said it, and he was given a standing ovation, a genuine spontaneous standing ovation at the end. So people can be made to accept things they don't want to hear. That is the other half of leadership. Mrs Thatcher is going to need both halves if she is to succeed in her nearly impossible task.

I would like to claim that I also had, and expressed, misgivings over Sir Geoffey Howe's watershed 1981 budget. But at the time I accepted the argument that it was right to switch taxation from earning to spending; and that it was part of a process which would make British industry leaner and fitter.

My head told me that I must support the policies which Mrs Thatcher was offering to force Britain on to its feet. But my heart still yearned for a different kind of conservatism. As I told the Conservative students at University College, Cardiff, in December 1982, 'Mrs Thatcher's Conservative Party is not the party which I joined in 1962, and I'm not at all sure that I like it. But Britain in 1982 is not the Britain of 1962; and I don't think that the change has been for the better'. But I had to accept that Harold Macmillan – and it was only because of Harold Macmillan that I had joined the Conservative Party – had paid too high a price, by allowing inefficient old ways to run on, in order to ensure national consensus.

I had to admit that the modernisation of Britain's creaking economy was now a task so urgent that it would have to take priority over national unity. Because of that overriding need I had to swallow my distaste for Mrs Thatcher's abrasiveness, her strident nationalism, her seeming lack of concern for the unemployed whose numbers were beginning to creep up alarmingly.

Above all, as a proclaimed moderate, a devotee of One Nation Toryism, I had to accept, at any rate temporarily, the end of the consensus which had held through alternations of Conservative and Labour Governments since 1945. For Mrs Thatcher, consensus means defeatism; it is a dirty word. She chooses to ignore the fact that it was her hero Winston Churchill who inaugurated the post-war consensus when he deliberately decided in 1951 not to reverse the huge social changes of the 1945 Attlee Government.

I felt at that time that I had no choice but to accept this sea change, though I could have no illusions as to what it would mean for such as myself. In Yeats's words:

The Centre cannot hold
The best lack all conviction
And the worst are full of passionate intensity.

But these troubles lay some way ahead. In the meantime I could concentrate on my love affair with my constituency. Of course there were occasional tiffs; and each year at the Annual General Meeting of the Conservative Committee at the delightful village of Cilcain, perched on the slopes of Moel Famau, we had a real ding-dong of fierce argument which was thoroughly enjoyed by all. But I seemed to be set for a reasonably quiet life in one of the safer seats until the time should come for me to retire, some time in the 1990s, having given twenty-five years or so of service to my constituents as Nigel Birch had done before me.

And then, out of a clear sky, lightning struck.

# CHAPTER EIGHT

# The Falklands Factor

## 1981–1982

In June 1981 the Boundary Commission published their proposals for alterations to the Parliamentary constituencies in Wales. Clwyd, as the fastest-growing county in Wales, was to have an additional, fifth seat.

A glance at the map of constituencies showed how simply this could have been done. A well-balanced, reasonably homogeneous and compact seat could have been carved out of the three existing seats in the Mold–Wrexham area; each of the three seats affected would have lost 15,000 to 20,000 electors, which would have brought them down to just below the national average; and the new seat would have been of similar size.

That was the solution which the Conservatives in Clwyd, supported by the Labour Party in Wrexham, put forward. But the Boundary Commission would have none of it. Their proposal was to skew the whole political map of Clwyd anticlockwise, so as to destroy three of the four existing constituencies, and to end up with a fifth constituency which had no recognisable identity.

The proposals of the Boundary Commission for the other counties of Wales were equally inept; but in every other county they were forced by public ridicule to abandon their proposals. In Clwyd they were not to be shifted.

It was not just the crassness of the Commission's proposals which was so deplorable; it was their ignorant insensitivity. Under their proposals there would no longer be a seat called Flint, nor one called Denbigh; instead we were to have Clwyd North West and Clwyd South West. Members of Parliament for Flint and for Denbigh have sat in the House of Commons continuously since 1547. Indeed the first parliament in which the Members for Flint and for Denbigh took their seats was the last one in which the Member for Calais sat. I am strongly opposed to capital punishment, but I would cheerfully restore it for Boundary Commissioners!

The Boundary Commissioners' proposals, if they were implemented as they stood (and they eventually were), were clearly going to present me with a major problem. My constituency was to be cut in two nearly equal halves; and at the appropriate moment I would have to decide which half I was going to stay with. To make matters more complicated there was no certainty that the changes would be brought into effect before the next election.

A cloud of uncertainty therefore hung over my future as an MP. Then a much bigger complication arose.

On 2 April 1982 Argentine forces landed on, and seized control of, the Falkland Islands. On 3 April, which was a Saturday, the House of Commons was called to emergency session. I was in my constituency. It was the day of my regular advice bureau, and I had a full programme of engagements which I decided not to break. After all, there was nothing I could have achieved at Westminster, and there were people in North Wales I did not want to let down.

The debate in the Commons was broadcast live. I heard a good deal of it between engagements; my wife heard pretty well all of it. Our reaction was spontaneous and identical. It seemed to both of us – and, rereading the debate, it still seems to me today – that the reaction of the Commons was so lacking in balanced judgement as to be not far short of hysteria. I had expected anger, I had expected resolve to put matters right; and I have to say that in both these respects the attitude of the Prime Minister herself was beyond criticism. But what I found sickening and repulsive were the backbench demands from both sides of the House, and from the Liberal benches too, for a scapegoat: the accusations of treachery directed against the Foreign Office and the Defence Ministry, and the call for the resignation of Lord Carrington, by far the most successful of Mrs Thatcher's Ministers. Perhaps the most frightening moment of all came when Mr Ray Whitney, a staunch Tory right-winger, pleaded for dispassionate consideration of the situation, as one who knew the Argentine well; he was promptly rounded on by the entire House as one who refused to join in the witch hunt, and was condemned by every subsequent speaker and by all press commentators for, at the very least, 'misjudging the mood of the House'.

Among my constituents that afternoon and evening, I found no trace of the madness which had swept through the House of Commons like a firestorm. Of course they were angry over the treacherous behaviour of the Argentines, and they welcomed, as I did, the announcement that a Task Force would sail for the South Atlantic in the next few days. However, like me they thought it inconceivable, and indeed wrong, that we should actually go to war, 8,000 miles away, on this issue. They hoped, as I did, that the Task Force would be used to strengthen our diplomatic position so as to enable us to negotiate an Argentine withdrawal; and, if that failed, perhaps to make the kind of unopposed landing that they made in South Georgia.

That day I was, I am sure, much closer to the mood of my constituents, than was the feverish House of Commons. In the days that followed, the atmosphere became notably more bellicose, largely because of the crude exploitation of the issue by sections of Fleet Street, most dishonourably *The Sun*, who realised what this could do for their circulations. But I saw no reason to alter my initial judgement. To my mind there was not one guilty Minister or government department; there were 635 guilty MPs who, every time they had been asked to consider the implications of the Falkland Islands' growing economic dependence on Argentina, Argentina's increasingly strident insistence that the Islands belonged to her, and the complete impossibility for Britain, 8,000 miles away, to provide permanent and effective deterrence against Argentine aggression, or even the investment to ensure the continued economic viability of the Islands – every time the Commons was put face to face with these awkward questions, it ran away from them muttering darkly about a 'sell out'. Of course the Foreign Office Ministers were to blame for not rubbing the noses of the MPs in it. However, a glance at Hansard for 2 December 1980, when Nicholas Ridley, then Minister of State at the FCO, tried to get the House to face up to the necessity for some kind of deal with the Argentines to ensure a secure future for the Falkland Islanders, and was hooted out of court by Sir Bernard Braine (Con), Russell Johnston (Lib), Julian Amery (Con), Donald Stewart (Scot. Nat), Tom Macnally (then Lab, later SDP), Douglas Jay (Lab), William Shelton (Con), David Lambie (Lab), Peter Shore from the Labour Front Bench, with a Parthian shot from John Farr (Con), should suffice to convince anyone that the House of Commons was not then, or for years afterwards, prepared to listen to common sense on this matter.

When I got back to London on 5 April, I went to see Michael Jopling, the Chief Whip. I told him of my views. I told him that although I supported the sending of the task force I could not undertake to support its use in the kind of opposed landing which could cause a heavy loss of life. I also told him that I would not make my doubts public without giving him advance warning. Michael received me kindly and courteously, but he told me he was 'shocked beyond measure' by my attitude.

On 14 April there was to be a further House of Commons debate on the Falklands. I now had to decide whether I should voice my doubts in public. I was under no illusion as to the probable consequences for me if I did speak out. By this time public opinion had swung almost entirely in favour of all forms of military action; and the Government had the full and virtually unqualified support of the Labour Party and the Alliance. Only the extreme left wing of the Labour Party stood out against, plus two or three individuals whose sturdy independence is regarded by some of their more conformist colleagues as exhibitionism – in other words, Tam Dalyell and Andrew Faulds. And, unlike the left-wing Labour MPs, I was facing a critically uncertain future in my constituency. On the other hand, what was I in politics for? Surely I was there because I passionately believe in certain things. It was, after all, because I believed in a united Europe, and in my country playing its part in that united Europe, that I had come into politics in the first place. Of course politics cannot always be a matter of passionate conviction; much of the time through party loyalty, or sometimes through sheer ignorance of the issues, one is supporting policies in which one has but the shallowest belief, or no interest at all. Furthermore, I am not often absolutely convinced that I am right on any political issue; I find it all too easy to see my opponent's point of view.

But on this issue I had no doubts; and my wife, who often counsels caution, was on this issue, as in the subsequent battle of Clwyd, in total agreement. I could do nothing other than voice my doubts, and voice them in the debate on 14 April.

I therefore went to see the Chief Whip once more, and told him that I was now going to do what I said I would do. I took a note to the Speaker, saying that I wanted to speak in the debate, and telling him of the line I would be taking. During the morning of the debate I ran into Jack Weatherill, then Deputy Speaker, in the corridor, and told him how anxious I was to speak, and why. And then I rang the North Wales Press Agency, run by my former Constituency chairman, Mike McEvoy, and gave him a press release giving the gist of my speech.

The debate was a more rational affair than the 3 April one had been. I was in my place on the fourth bench above the gangway throughout. Every time a member finished his contribution I stood up to catch the Speaker's eyes. He did not seem to notice me. About 6pm the Chief Whip came and sat beside me, and begged me, insistently but quite kindly, not to speak. It seemed to me perfectly proper for the Chief Whip to put pressure on me in this way, and I went a quarter of the way to meet him by promising both to give support to the sending of the task force and to the taking of such military action as was necessary for its own defence. Only very slightly relieved, the Chief Whip left me. I continued to rise in my place; the Speaker continued not to notice me. Perhaps a lot of members had put in a request to speak; though when I had put in my request to the Speaker's office I had been told that at that stage there were very few. Then one of my Conservative colleagues was called. He began his speech, 'Mr Speaker, when I came into this debate this afternoon I had no intention of taking part . . .'. Clearly something had gone wrong. Mr

Speaker Thomas always made it clear that he very much disliked Members coming up to him when he was in the Chair and asking about their chances of being called to speak (for you can only speak in the House of Commons if, after you have risen in your place, the Speaker calls your name). Clearly I would have to risk the Speaker's displeasure. I sidled up to his Chair. 'Did you not get my note, Mr Speaker, saying that I wanted to speak, and why?' Mr Speaker looked at me, kindly as ever, but clearly embarrassed, 'I'm sorry, Anthony, I thought you had changed your mind. I'll call you next but one'. And he did. By that time it was getting towards the time for the final winding up speeches, so the House was a good deal fuller for what most of them considered a shocking performance than it would have been earlier.

Of course I was nervous. It is intensely painful saying things which upset one's friends; and I could hear Tony Buck and John Eden near me audibly upset by what I was saying; I like and admire them both. But I was not too nervous to say exactly what I wanted to say. I did not give way, as in normal circumstances I would have done, to those on my side, in particular Alan Clarke, who tried to interrupt me.

The speech was not long, so perhaps I can quote it more or less in full.

6.20 pm

Sir Anthony Meyer (Flint, West): I have set myself a hard and disagreeable task that has been made harder and more disagreeable by the wise speeches with which the debate was opened, particularly by the very balanced and judicious speech of my right hon. Friend the Prime Minister.

I shall say two things that will be distasteful to both

sides of the House. The first is that I believe that the clamour that the House set up on 3 April for the resignation of Lord Carrington marked one of the lowest points in its history. Lord Carrington's offence was to believe in the absolute necessity to reach some kind of agreement with the Argentines over the Falklands, since to defend them against a hostile neighbour in perpetuity would be prohibitively costly. Events will prove him right.

The House did itself no honour by echoing the hysterical demands in the press that national humiliation should be purged by offering a scapegoat. My right hon. Friend the present Foreign Secretary is a man of outstanding ability and total integrity, but with Lord Carrington we have lost the Minister who could best have turned to our advantage the initial prejudice of world opinion in our favour – a prejudice that his diplomatic skill had done so much to create. Clearly, the strongest card in our hand is the whole-hearted support of the EEC. I hope that hon. Members on both sides will note that.

The second and still more distasteful thing I must do is question some part of the consensus in this House, excluding only far Left and the hon. Members for West Lothian (Mr. Dalyell) and for South Ayrshire (Mr. Foulkes), about what to do next.

The Government have, rightly, the unanimous support of the House for the two propositions that the Argentines must not be allowed to enjoy undisturbed the fruits of their wanton and unprovoked aggression, and that the people of the Falkland Islands must recover their right of self-determination. They have the overwhelming support of this House for the proposition that it is both right and expedient to dispatch the task force to demonstrate the firmness of our resolve and to use that task force, if need be, to enforce a blockade. I am part of that consensus, although not without misgivings caused by the gap that is now left in our defences against our real enemy – the Soviet Union.

There is also overwhelming support on both sides of the House for the proposition that we should seek a peaceful solution to the crisis, but that if diplomacy fails we must be ready to use force to restore British sovereignty or, at any rate, British administration to the islands. I have to tell my right hon. Friends with great sadness, having given many hours of agonising thought to the matter, that I for one on this side – and, perhaps, only for one – am not part of that consensus.

I do not believe that it would be right, I do not believe that it would in the end help us to achieve our objectives, to use force in such a way as to kill people, Service men or civilians, just to ensure that the Union Jack – the Union Jack alone – flies over what would be left of public buildings in the Falklands.

If there is fighting, there will be casualties – British casualties and, indeed, Welsh casualties – on both sides. Some casualties may be unavoidable from the very presence of the task force in those waters. Of course, if the Argentines attack we must defend ourselves. That risk is real if we establish a blockade.

I accept that risk. What I cannot accept is that the task force should at any time be given instructions to seek out and destroy Argentine vessels or installations or to attempt an opposed landing in circumstances where substantial casualties are to be expected.

If the Government really intend – as reports in *The*

*Times* today suggest, and contrary to the impression
given by the Prime Minister in her opening speech – to
carry matters as far as that, I have no doubt that they
will have the overwhelming support of this House,
certainly of Conservative Members and of the majority
of Opposition Members. I must tell them that at that
stage they will no longer have mine.

It did not create quite as much stir as I had expected, though
the BBC *Today in Parliament* carried an extract and the
midnight news reported that mine had been the sole Conservative voice critical of the Government. It was the subsequent
*Panorama* interview which created the storm. But before I
come to that, perhaps I might complete the story of the
Speaker and the Invisible Member.

Why had the Speaker, whose job it is to safeguard the
interests of minorities and to ensure that all points of view are
expressed, tried so hard not to call me? It was of course
impossible that he should not have seen me standing up each
time a speech ended. It was surely inconceivable that the Chief
Whip could have exerted any pressure on the Speaker not to
call me, as he had exerted pressure on me not to speak. That,
unlike the pressure on me, would have been grossly improper.
It would have been still more improper for the Speaker to
have given in to such pressure; and I must make it quite clear
that I do not believe for one moment that such pressure was
exerted by the Chief Whip, or that the Speaker would have
accepted it. I thought I ought to try to find out, so I sent a
note to the Speaker, courteous but worried, and asked to see
him. He saw me straight away and, as usual, overwhelmed me
with his charm and kindness. He said that he had made a
mistake, that in the light of hindsight he would have acted

differently, that he had been concerned for the consequences for me, and a lot more besides.

What was the real reason? I don't really know. But I think I can guess. George Thomas was a great Speaker, certainly the greatest since World War II, perhaps the greatest of this century. He was also a great, indeed a slightly narrow, patriot. He had an obsessive dislike of both Welsh Nationalism and of European integration, both of which he saw as destructive to the nation state. As Speaker, he found it perfectly possible to accommodate his views with the anti-nationalist views of the extreme left; what threw him off-balance was to have such views expressed by people who were in the centre of the political spectrum. In addition he had an immense, indeed uncritical admiration for Mrs Thatcher's leadership. It may possibly be that the combination of these two factors led him to the conclusion that he had the right and the duty to ensure that the House of Commons demonstrated national unity in support of the Prime Minister at a time of national crisis; and that if there were to be any dissentient voices they should come from the extreme left alone. In other words, he put his duty to the nation before his duty to Parliament. And who will dare to say he was wrong? Not I; but remember that the President of the Reichstag could have made the same plea.

There were, of course, reactions to my Commons speech in my constituency. My agent, Wilf Storey, a man of endless loyalty, told me that he was getting a substantial although not huge number of calls; they were about evenly divided between friendly and hostile. He thought it would help if I came up specially to Wales the following Thursday to attend a meeting of the West Flint Conservative Association Executive at the tiny village of Gorsedd. I went. He was right. The meeting was a little disorderly, critical of me, but not really hostile. A motion was passed, thanks largely to Wilf Storey's skill, strongly supporting the Government, but also approving my efforts to ensure minimum loss of life. I am sure that a certain number of those at that meeting, particularly from the heartland of the new Delyn constituency, came to the conclusion that this time my left-of-centre views had carried me too far, and that they would do what they could to ensure that I was not readopted. What I found a little sad was that a number, mainly ladies, came up to me after the meeting, saying that they entirely agreed with me but hadn't dared say so.

A larger time-bomb was ticking away under me. Soon after my Commons speech, BBC *Panorama* rang up. Would I, with a number of other MPs, be interviewed in depth on the Falklands issue? Of course I had to accept. The interviews were carefully conducted in a broiling Commons Committee room. Mine must have lasted for twenty-five minutes. David Crouch, who had expressed misgivings similar to mine, was also interviewed. So, of course, was Tam Dalyell.

The *Panorama* programme, entitled 'The Falklands; the Voice of Dissent', went out on 10 May. It caused a storm of fury, throughout the country and within the Conservative Party. The trouble was that, in addition to the doubts and anxieties expressed by David Crouch and myself, it contained specific and detailed criticisms by Tam Dalyell of the military soundness of the operation, supported by allegations that some of the most senior RAF officers were strongly opposed to the enterprise, on the grounds that it was madness to risk so large a force and so many sea-borne troups within 400 miles of the Argentine mainland, without proper air cover. These allegations completely unbalanced the programme so that, instead of sounding a note of hesitant doubt, it became an attack on the Government's policy. Indeed, it came perilously close to accusing Mrs Thatcher of gambling with lives in order to strengthen her political posture. I believe this charge to be totally devoid of foundation, and I said so at the time. On the other hand, I could not possibly complain that my own contribution to the programme, which had been boiled down from 20 minutes to a couple of 2-minute excerpts, was anything other than a completely fair representation of what I had said. I deplored the programme as a whole; I had to admit that my own contribution to it was in no way a misrepresentation. I said as much to the crowded meeting of the Conservative Backbench Media Committee which met on 12 May to discuss with, or rather to pillory, the Chairman of the BBC, George Howard, and the Director General, Alistair Milne. These two distinguished men, neither of whom could possibly be regarded as unfriendly to the Conservative Party, were treated like criminals by speaker after speaker. My own contribution to the discussion was, as a matter of fact, quite well received; but the meeting as a whole was the verbal equivalent of a lynching party.

There was no doubt that I had deeply offended many Conservatives, inside Parliament and without; not merely by what I had myself said on the programme, but because I was part of a programme which seemed to be stabbing the Government in the back in the middle of military operations. Two senior backbenchers came up to me in the smoking room and said that they no longer regarded me as a colleague.

On the other hand there were a number, including some on the right wing of the Party, notably John Stokes and Nick Budgen, who went out of their way to show me personal friendship at this time. I was in no way surprised that the Deputy Speaker, now Mr Speaker himself, Jack Weatherill, took the trouble to send me a kind, and very helpful message; but I was surprised, delighted and impressed to receive a letter on 10 Downing Street notepaper, from the Prime Minister's PPS, Ian Gow, saying, 'I disagreed with every word you said, but I salute your courage in saying it'.

I would like to add three footnotes. At the time I was bitterly critical of the decision to sink the *General Belgrano* when she was well outside the war zone and steaming away from the Falklands. In retrospect I have to acknowledge that the Prime Minister had no choice but to order the submarine *Conqueror* to sink her; the *Belgrano* constituted a potential threat to the lives of British servicemen who were in action at her decision; and she would not have been justified in neglecting any measure needful to enhance their safety.

But the sinking of the *Belgrano*, and the gloating with which the news was received by much of the media, reminded me of a story from the last war when a newsreel was shown in a crowded Glasgow cinema of the sinking by the Navy of the German cruiser, the *Graf Spee*. The whole audience broke into loud applause; but as the cheering died down a woman's voice was heard, 'Aye, and there's a thousand wives and mothers that will never see their menfolk again'.

The second is of greater consequence. Although I was unhappy, not so much about the Falklands operation as about the popular mood surrounding it, I have become increasingly convinced that the Prime Minister was right to send the Task Force, and to order it to recapture the Islands; not so much in order to protect the Islanders' right to choose their status as to show the world that aggression does not always pay.

The third reflection concerns the Service of Remembrance held in St Paul's Cathedral after the campaign. The Archbishop of Canterbury, as may be remembered, insisted that it be a service of reconciliation, and included prayers for the Argentinian casualties and their relatives. Mrs Thatcher was furious; reconciliation is not a word that figures in her vocabulary. She had wanted a celebration of glorious victory. From that day on the Archbishop was added to the lengthening list of her enemies.

My own admiration for the Archbishop was already great, and was further increased by this determination to uphold Christian values in the face of steady pressure to bend to the will of the Iron Lady. As for myself I received what seemed to me at the time a fairly large mail on the stand I had taken, some 150 letters; they ran about 4 to 1 in my favour. Although most of them came from people who were clearly not Conservatives, of the Conservatives who wrote to me rather more supported me than attacked me. A few of the attacks were virulent. One seems to deserve quotation for its classical elegance. It was a telegram which ran:

SIR ANTHONY MYER
HOUSE OF COMMONS
LONDON

I REMEMBER YOU AT ETON AND YOUR MOTHER
AT DATCHET.
IN MY OPINION YOU DISGRACE OUR SCHOOL
YOUR REGIMENT AND MY COUNTRY

Another was rather harder to categorise:

Sir Anthony Meyer M.P.
House of Commons.

Dear Sir,
    After watching you on television with your weak and frightened face and opposed to England's stand against

Argentine – I suggest you resign your seat to enable
another Conservative to take over.

If you are not with this Government, you must be
against it and that means you support Argentine.

I hope your house is burgled (if I was a young man I
would do it) all your belongings are stolen and your
wife, or daughter is raped as the Falkland Islander's have
been by the Argentines. I pray there is one young
Englishman about to take over the task – we had lots in
my younger days during the 1939–45 war.

       I wish you to hell

Copy to: The Prime Minister
(Mrs M. Thatcher) Get rid of this 'Judus' in our
England.

What was remarkable was how few of the letters came from
within the constituency. Nonetheless, it was clear that I had
created for myself a fresh and formidable obstacle to my
readoption.

# CHAPTER NINE

# The Battle
# for Clwyd

## Part 1
## The Triumph
## of Miss Brookes

### 1982–1983

In the meantime the process of electoral boundary change in Clwyd rolled inexorably on; it also became increasingly likely that the General Election would be held in 1983 rather than in 1984. I was therefore going to have to choose which of the two new constituencies containing part of my existing one I was going to stay with. Although the eastern half, which would constitute the heartland of the new Delyn constituency, was slightly the larger, it contained rather more of those party workers who had been deeply upset by my Falklands stand; whereas in Rhyl, which was to go into the new Clwyd North West constituency, and which was the largest town in my old constituency, there appeared to be a deep well of sympathy and support for my wife and me.

I therefore made up my mind to go for the Clwyd North

West seat. Obviously I would have to contend with the sitting member for Denbigh, Geraint Morgan, an able, Welsh-speaking lawyer. He too was having to make a choice; the other half of his constituency was being turned into the hugely cumbrous new Clwyd South West seat, a largely Welsh-speaking rural area. Although he would have been very welcome to stand there (and would certainly have won the seat), he turned it down in favour of the much safer Clwyd North West.

I was therefore faced with a straight fight with Geraint Morgan, unless the selection committee were to include an outsider. This, of course, is what they ought to have done. The new seat was certain to be the safest Tory seat in Wales; and it should then, and should now, be held by a youngish politician of outstanding talent who could credibly fill the office of Secretary of State for Wales. That is what the Selection Committee should have done; but I felt pretty certain that they wouldn't. Four years earlier, the Tories of North Wales had had to choose their candidate for the North Wales seat in the European Parliament. They were not offered a wide choice of candidates; but their first act was to eliminate the one candidate of real talent who presented himself, Peter Price. I felt reasonably certain they would do the same again, and I was right.

I felt that I stood a very fair chance of beating Geraint Morgan, despite the Falklands millstone hanging round my neck. It is fair to say that I was, and was widely known to have been, very much more active both in Parliament and in my constituency than he, a busy lawyer and sitting recorder, had ever been.

Although I felt sure that there was little risk of intervention by a talented outsider, there was one potential candidate who was to be dreaded; the hyper-active, high profile, perfectly groomed Miss Beata Brookes, the North Wales MEP. She had one inestimable advantage over both Geraint Morgan and me; she could, and did, range freely through both our constituencies, whereas by strictly observed House of Commons convention Morgan could not operate in my constituency, nor I in his. It was therefore a great relief to have Miss Brookes's assurance that she had no intention of seeking nomination for Clwyd North West, and that her sole interest was in her Euro seat. This understanding was confirmed when the Tories of Clwyd South West, having failed to persuade Geraint Morgan to be their candidate, turned to Miss Brookes, who firmly declined; Europe was her sole interest.

The Selection Committee met on 17 February 1983. They had before them a list of sixty-seven names submitted in accordance with Conservative Central Office rules, and Mr Morgan's name and mine. They decided, as I had expected, to reject out of hand all the outside names sent in; and were about to vote on a proposition that only two names be considered, when the Chairman announced that he had received a letter proposing Miss Brookes, that he had taken the precaution of telephoning her before the meeting, and had obtained her consent to being nominated.

Miss Brookes was born and brought up in the constituency, and had held high office in the local Conservative Association. She certainly had the right to put in a bid for the nomination; but her intervention did raise some very awkward issues.

There was certainly something richly ironic about her entry into the lists against me. I had become famous, indeed notorious at Westminster for my championship of the cause of MEPs who were then, and to a lesser extent still are, treated by MPs as second-class citizens, to be sent round to the tradesmen's entrance should they be so presumptuous as to present themselves at the front door. This was all of the piece with my strong support for the cause of European integration, which had always been and still is my top priority in politics. I had, indeed, founded a series of *al fresco* lunchtime meetings which were the only occasions on which MPs and MEPs ever met together to discuss matters of common concern. Miss Brookes herself had actually attended one of these lunchtime meetings.

Some of my anti-European colleagues derived mischievous pleasure from the fact that I, the acknowledged champion of the MEPs, should now be challenged for the nomination in my own seat by an MEP from my own party. I could see the funny side of it. But it did also raise rather serious issues over the trust which is needed between MPs and MEPs of the same party in the same area. MPs have to be at Westminster all week; and it would be worrying to feel that the MEP might be prowling around their constituency during that time trying to usurp their support.

So Miss Brookes had the advantage of being in the constituency at times when Mr Morgan and I could not be there. As I have explained, she could range freely through both our constituencies. On top of that the agent who was organising the selection contest was also her Euro-agent; and the contest was being organised from the same office as her office. On top of that again, it was well known by now that the Chairman was well disposed towards Miss Brookes's candidature. All in all this did not look much like the recipe for a fair and equal contest. There was only to be a bare two weeks from the decision to include Miss Brookes's name to the meeting of the large Selection Committee which was to choose between us. There clearly was no time for me to set about identifying support in the Denbigh end of the constituency, always supposing that Mr Morgan would have been ready to allow me to do so, which he was not.

All I could do was to draw the attention of the press and broadcasting to what was going on; and to try to get the Conservative Party at the top level to step in and insist on a fair contest. I succeeded admirably with the media; but the top brass in the Conservative Party, apart from the Conservative Chief Whip in the European Parliament, Christopher Prout, became less and less helpful. They wanted me to go without making a fuss. The Secretary of State for Wales, Nicholas Edwards, told me quite bluntly that I ought to give up the fight, and that Miss Brookes was certain to win. The Party Chairman, Cecil Parkinson, asked me to see him at Central Office and suggested that I should try for a European seat instead. I spent nearly two hours in Cecil's office that afternoon. It was during the critical Darlington by-election, and messages from the front kept pouring in and interrupting our conversation. I was able to form my own opinion of the way in which he handled his job as Party Chairman. I have to say that I felt as if I had strayed into the servants' hall of a not very well run stately home, rather than the nerve centre of a great political party at a critical stage in its battle for supremacy. I also reflected on how very differently Lord Thorneycroft, the previous Party Chairman, would have handled the interview with me. I am sure he would have had me round to lunch at White's, oysters and champagne, a lot of talk about how he was sure I would understand the needs of the Party at a time like this, a vague suggestion that there would be all sorts of ways in which I could render great service to the state in some other place, and I would have come away from the lunch, quite possibly having agreed to stand down, or, if not, feeling that I was behaving like a cad.

*Autre temps, autres moeurs.* Mrs Thatcher had the Party Chairman she wanted and deserved. I left the meeting with Cecil Parkinson with renewed determination to fight on.

It was now only four days to the meeting of the Selection Committee; four days during which I had been busy at the House of Commons, and Miss Brookes free to canvass support in the constituency and further strengthen her position.

Moreover, the selection was to take place behind closed doors at a time and a place to be kept secret. The consequences would have been twofold: Miss Brookes would win easily, but no one would believe that she had won fairly. After all, the Committee was choosing, not just the Conservative candidate, but in effect the Member of Parliament for this ultra-safe Tory seat. It seemed to me then, it still seems to me now, that in such cases secret selection procedures are inadmissible.

I therefore decided to drag the whole thing out into the daylight, and to secure the maximum publicity. I told my story to Julian Haviland of *The Times*, and to David Rose of the *Liverpool Daily Post*, and they ensured that it received good coverage. I was trying to expose the dubious features of the selection process, and to force the powers-that-be in the Conservative Party to ensure a selection procedure in Clwyd North West which would be seen to be equitable, and which would go a little way to diminishing the unfair advantage which Miss Brookes enjoyed in consequence of her status as the Euro-member, with the lavish opportunities which it gave her for regular contact with Party workers throughout the constituency. It was a forlorn hope. The fortnight which elapsed between Miss Brookes's sudden entry on the scene and the start of the selection process was too short to enable such a radical departure from normal selection procedures even to be seriously considered.

It was quite clear that there was no chance that the result of the Selection Committee meeting would be accepted by the public as being fair or above board. All I could do was to cry 'Foul!' very loudly before the meeting; it would have been no good doing so afterwards, even though by thus exciting publicity I further damaged my chances at the meeting.

The Selection Committee meeting was held on Sunday, 6 March. As I had expected Miss Brookes emerged the winner; but not as easily as I had expected. Indeed, on the first round of voting I had 35 votes, she had 28, and Mr Morgan had 14. But on the second ballot (and the fact that there had to be a second ballot turned out to be of crucial importance) all but one of Mr Morgan's votes switched from Mr Morgan, whom they knew, to Miss Brookes whom they also knew; so Miss Brookes won by 41 votes to 36.

There was a good deal of media interest in the result, but it did not last long. The next day was the monthly Welsh Question day in the House of Commons. There was a question about a recent road accident in the village of Bodelwyddan in my constituency, in which two children had been run over and killed; an incident which Miss Brookes, who lived in the village, had managed to make good use of for publicity purposes. Leo Abse intervened to ask what the Secretary of State was going to do about the two Conservative MPs who had been run over by the Conservative Party machine in North Wales; a good joke, but not specially helpful. Then I rose to remind Nicholas Edwards, the Secretary of State, of the support which I had always given him, and to seek his assurance that he was not involved in the attempt to unseat me. This intervention, which was certainly not in order, roused the ire of the Speaker, who normally was pretty indulgent in allowing members to stray from the point provided that they did not take up too much time; and he ordered me quite roughly to sit down; perhaps he still remembered with displeasure how I had stepped out of line on the Falklands.

By 18 March, two weeks after the Selection Committee meeting, my wife and I had pretty well given up hope. Miss

Brookes had been selected for adoption; the adoption machinery was firmly in the hands of a chairman and an agent who were working solely for her; and there was no way in which I could now halt the inexorable process, which clearly had the full weight of the party machine behind it.

We had many good friends in the constituency urging me to go on; one particularly jolly message from a local Catholic priest ran, 'I am praying like stink that your adversary gets the staggers, and I am distributing small waxen images and plenty of pins to the more right-minded of my parishioners'. However, the difficulties seemed insurmountable. I could not make contact with the party members in the Denbigh part of the constituency, because the agent, on instructions from the Chairman, refused to let me have the list. My last forlorn hope was to persuade the General Meeting of the Conservative Association, which according to the rules had to be called to refuse to endorse the Selection Committee's choice; but this General Meeting kept on being put off on one pretext after another; and in the meantime the imminence of the General Election loomed ever larger. Once the Election was called it would be too late to consider rejecting the Selection Committee's choice. It seemed pretty well hopeless.

And then, on Sunday, 17 April, after a British Legion Service in St Asaph Cathedral at which I had been skilfully upstaged by Miss Brookes, my eye lighted on a report tucked away at the bottom of a column in *The Sunday Times*. It was headed 'Clwyd is fluid again' and it was written by James Tucker. A new door had opened.

# CHAPTER TEN

# The Battle
# for Clwyd

# Part 2
# The Rule
# of Law

## 1983

James Tucker's article in *The Sunday Times* of 17 April drew a parallel between what had happened earlier in the week at Bridgend and the situation in Clwyd North West. At the Selection Committee meeting for Bridgend there was a voting tie between the local candidate, Peter Hubbard Miles, and a strong contender from outside. Instead of sending both these candidates through to a final adoption meeting, and allowing that meeting to choose between them, there was a second ballot at which the Chairman used his casting vote, and Peter Hubbard Miles was defeated by one vote. Conservative Central Office showed an almost indecent haste to endorse the result.

Hubbard Miles was not taking this lying down. He consulted a particularly bright local solicitor, who consulted

Counsel in Cardiff. What had been done at Bridgend apeared to be contrary to the Bridgend Conservative Association's own rules, which provided that 'In the event of no candidate receiving an overall majority . . . the Executive Council shall recommend more than one candidate for consideration by a General Meeting.' The case was heard in the High Court in London, and settled out, but only just out, of court. Lawyers representing the Bridgend Conservative Association agreed that the General Meeting could accept nominations from the floor, even though they had had no recommendation from the Executive Council.

James Tucker's article drew an analogy between what had happened in Bridgend, and the situation in Clwyd North West, and suggested that there, too, it might be that nominations from the floor would have to be accepted.

The first thing for me to do was to ring Peter Hubbard Miles and get the name of his solicitor. The next day we travelled to Bridgend; the solicitor already knew a good deal about the case, and rang Counsel in Cardiff. Yes, there was an analogy between my case and Peter Hubbard Miles's. I could seek an injunction requiring either that my name be put to the General Meeting, since there had been no overall majority in the first ballot of the Selection Committee, or, alternatively, that nominations should be accepted from the floor. After lengthy discussion with Counsel, John Griffiths Williams, we decided to go ahead.

Senior Conservatives at Westminster took two different views of my now well-publicised decision to go to law. There were those who told me that it was a catastrophic mistake to sue my own Association. I was half inclined to agree. But I was told that, in view of what had happened at Bridgend, the Clwyd North West Association would be advised to settle out of court, and to agree to accept nominations from the floor of the General Meeting.

The Clwyd North West Steering Committee, however, decided to ignore this advice, and to contest the matter in court.

The Court Hearing was for 10.30 am on Friday, 6 May. The local elections had been held the previous day. They did not give Mrs Thatcher quite the clear message to go ahead that she had been hoping for; but they were not discouraging enough to provide her with any excuse for disappointing the expectations which had been allowed to build up. No one could doubt that the election would be announced within three days; the only uncertainty was whether polling day would be 9 June or 23 June.

When the Judge, Mr Justice Caulfield, came in he made it plain that he was aware of the political significance of the case. He then went on to say that in view of the public importance of the matter he was surprised that the hearing was to be in chambers. He recommended that it would be in open court, with the press present; and furthermore that instead of seeking interim relief, we should seek a definitive ruling. He added that, in view of the obvious time factor, and to meet the possibility of an appeal, he had arranged for the Court of Appeal to stand by for a hearing later that day if need be.

I had been keen for my counsel to put in a double plea; and, against his better judgement, he had agreed to do so. We therefore argued that the Selection Committee, having failed to get an absolute majority for any candidate on the first ballot, should have sent the names, not of one, but of the two leading contenders to the adoption meeting. The second plea was that since this meeting was in fact the first Annual General Meeting of the new Constituency Association, it could not be denied the right, if it chose, to accept nominations from the floor, even though there was no provision for this in the agenda for the meeting, which had been printed and which spoke merely of 'The adoption of Miss Beata Brookes, MEP, as Parliamentary candidate'.

I had a very good reason for wanting to secure the possibility of nominations from the floor. It would have enabled Geraint Morgan to be nominated. If I, by taking legal action at my own expense, could win this right for Morgan, then surely that would disarm criticism that I was using the law in a manner injurious to my own Association, purely to secure my own political advantage. I therefore gave renewed instructions to counsel that he was to press this demand.

The move from chambers to open court meant that counsel had to send for his gown, and there was some forty minutes delay. As soon as we resumed after that, with the press sitting in the court, it became clear that the judge did not think much of the argument that nominations should be allowed from the floor. My wife gave me a nudge. I gave the solicitor a nudge. He leant over to counsel; and he, quick as a knife, withdrew the demand. In the nick of time. The judge was clearly much impressed with the rule in the procedure book which said that if there was no absolute majority, more than one name should be sent in to the final adoption meeting, and it was on this point that judgement was eventually given. In the meantime, my counsel had sat down, having made an excellent impression on the judge by the swiftness of his reactions to the judge's clearly signalled intention. Now it was the turn of counsel for the North West Clwyd Conservative Association. He made a bad start. Seeing that it was now twenty to one, he suggested a lunch break. The judge was not pleased. 'Nobody', he remarked severely, 'gets to lunch at Lincoln's Inn until 1 o'clock. We will continue till one.'

Evidently either the food or the company at the benchers'
lunch had been unsatisfactory; for the judge was in a very
terse mood after lunch; and counsel for the defendants, who
had set himself the impossible task of trying to prove that the
selection procedures had followed the rules to the letter, was
manifestly floundering before Mr Justice Caulfield's far from
indulgent eye. One of my friends in the press box gave me a
knowing look. We were going to win.

The judge did not need more than half an hour to ponder
his ruling. The passage in the model rules which runs 'if there
is no overall majority, then the Executive Council should
recommend more than one candidate for consideration by the
General Meeting' must mean that, unless the *first ballot* in the
Executive Council (i.e., the Selection Committee) produced
one candidate with an absolute majority, the Committee must
recommend more than one candidate; if not, then the stipula-
tion was meaningless, for it would always be possible eventually, by a series of eliminating ballots, to produce a candidate
with an absolute majority, and therefore no circumstances
could ever arise in which the General Meeting would have a
choice. He therefore ruled that in the present case the Selection
Committee should have sent not one, but two names for
consideration by the General Meeting; and that the North
West Clwyd Conservative Association should now make
arangements accordingly. Having found in favour of the
plaintiff (i.e., me), he then asked me if I wanted to claim costs.
My own costs had amounted to some £2,000; but it would
clearly have been folly to seek costs against what I hoped
would be my own Association; I therefore waived the judge's
offer, and said that I would pay my own costs.

Nothing was said about an appeal; so the judgement was
final. My wife and I walked out into the sunshine of the Strand
to face the television cameras, looking a good deal happier

than when we went in. We had won a battle, and an important one. But it could well prove a pyrrhic victory; would it not swing opinion in the constituency against me? Maybe; but now that the election was so obviously imminent the right to appear before the General Meeting was all important. That meeting was now going to have a choice between two candidates; not between one candidate and a void.

It was announced that morning from 10 Downing Street that the Election would be on 9 June; four weeks ahead. The General Meeting of the Clwyd North West Association, which had been called on Monday, 9 May, was therefore going to have not merely to pick a candidate from the two which were now on offer, but also formally to adopt that candidate for the General Election campaign which was starting that very day. And, as if that were not enough, it was also to be the first Annual General Meeting of the new Clwyd North West Conservative Association, and would have to elect its own officers before it could get down to business.

Kinmel Manor Hotel has a large car park, but not nearly large enough. It also has a very long and narrow drive. When we arrived we found that the car park was full, the drive was jammed with coaches, all of which seemed to have come from Colwyn Bay, and that we had to park nearly half a mile from the hotel. When we reached the hotel on foot, past all these large, unfriendly buses, we found a large, equally unfriendly queue of people, none of whom we knew, waiting to get in.

We had decided to have dinner at the hotel while the meeting was being prepared. This meant that we had to ease our way in through the large, unfriendly queue. We passed Geraint Morgan and his wife. I told him how sorry I was that I had been unable to win for him, as I had done for myself, the right to speak at this meeting. He told me that he intended to demand this right from the floor.

Dinner was a weird, dreamlike affair. Only two tables were occupied in the long dining-room. My wife and I sat at a table for two; beside us was a window in the inner wall through which we could see the bar, which in turn opened into the ballroom where first the Steering Committee meeting, and then the General Meeting, were being held. From time to time people waiting in the bar came up to the window and greeted us. The only other occupied table seated thirty people. At it were what appeared to be the world's press and TV. Every time we took a mouthful they took a photograph. They also treated us to their views. They were uniformly discouraging. 'It looks pretty bad for you', was the general theme. It was all very depressing.

The first break in the clouds came with the startling news that the Annual General Meeting, which had to precede the adoption meeting, had voted to replace the Chairman with one less hostile to my candidature. Although this was in itself good news, it also meant that there was no longer any possibility of me refusing to accept the further decisions of this meeting, since it was manifestly going to be conducted fairly. I would have to accept defeat as final, and all our efforts over the past weeks would have been in vain.

Miss Brookes and I had tossed a coin as to who should go first. She had won, and chose to speak second. When I was called to enter the meeting room, overcrowded and over-heated, the booing was a lot louder than the cheering.

I began with a tribute to Miss Brookes and the work she did for Wales in Europe, and for Europe in Wales. But I pointed out the impossibility of doing both jobs, in Europe and at Westminster. I referred to my work in my former constituency, touched on the Falklands affair, explaining that with my war record I was no pacifist, and made it plain that, loyal though I was to the Conservative Party, I would never surrender the right to speak my mind. The speech went down well. I did not have too much trouble with questions.

As I went out, to rather louder cheers and softer boos, I felt that I had done all I could to improve my chances; but that it was unlikely to be enough.

Miss Brookes went in, to much louder cheers than I had received. I am told that she gave the same speech as she had given to the Selection Committee, a ringing panegyric of Mrs Thatcher and of the Conservative Party. It was not quite what the audience wanted to hear. She had little to say about her policies or her political attitudes, and part of her audience became restive. She recovered herself during questions, until she was faced with this one, which underlay all the doubts which had subsisted since her candidature was announced: 'Miss Brookes, how are you going to find the time to look after this seat and your European one?' She replied, without hesitation, 'I will send a telegram tomorrow to Conservative Central Office asking them to make immediate arrangements for the choice of a new Euro-candidate, and I will resign my seat in the European Parliament forthwith'. And then came the fatal supplementary question: 'It costs £30,000 to fight a European by-election. Where are we going to find that kind of money?'

I understand that the final voting figures were something like 420 for me and 280 for Miss Brookes. She was gracious in defeat; and I gave her, to the joy of the press cameras and of Sir Robin Day, who interviewed me for the *World at One* the next day, a chaste peck on the cheek.

Our troubles were over for the time being. No one could be in any doubt of the result of the General Election which was now about to start, still less of the outcome in Clwyd North West. My task was not so much to win, and to do so with a large majority, as to heal the wounds within the local Conservative Association. This task was made easier by the election campaign coming so hard on the heels of the bloody battle for the nomination.

I worked harder during this election campaign, and so did my wife and many members of my family, than in any previous campaign, not excluding the two which I fought in hyper-marginal Eton and Slough in 1964 and 1966. The object was only secondarily to make an impression on the electors; the main object was to show the Conservative party workers that they had a candidate and a candidate's wife who would work them into the ground, walk them off their feet and still find time to be pleasant to them. At the same time we had in the course of three weeks to make the kind of contacts with local non-political organisations in the Colwyn Bay area which I had established over the years in Rhyl, to get on good terms with a new set of local papers, and to be seen around, all the time and everywhere.

For this purpose the fame, indeed notoriety, which I had acquired in the course of the past few weeks proved a positive asset. Every time I went into a pub or a shop I was recognised. By contrast the Liberal candidate, who had been nursing the seat for years, and who had kept a very low profile during the preceding period, not wanting to spoil the chances of Miss Brookes (the one Conservative candidate he thought he might beat), was at a corresponding disadvantage when the election campaign followed directly on the nomination battle, and he found that he had slipped from public memory.

In contrast to what had gone before, the election campaign was a low-profile and civilised affair, and I had good relations with all my opponents.

Since the night in October 1964 when I won Eton and Slough by 11 votes after three recounts I have always found the election count a slightly disagreeable anti-climax after the hard work of the campaign itself. This time, the long drawn-out affair at Colwyn Leisure Centre was no exception. There were a few moments of anxiety when we failed to observe that the Liberal candidate's votes were being stacked in bundles of 4,000, whereas mine were in bundles of 5,000, and it looked as if my majority was down to less than 5,000; and I was disappointed at the collapse of the Labour vote, which meant a further 3,000 or so votes for the Liberal, thus cutting my majority. And it would have been nice to go over the 10,000 mark, instead of missing it by 500 or so. But we had over 50 per cent of the poll; in that respect the best Conservative result in Wales.

CHAPTER ELEVEN

# The Thatcher
# Triumph

## 1983–1987

Throughout the general election campaign my concern had been not so much to win the seat as to heal the wounds which had been inflicted by the struggle for the nomination. It was good to know that the former Chairman's efforts, which seemed to have cost him the Chairmanship, had earned him an OBE in the dissolution honours; and that the agent had received an invitation to the Queen's Garden Party at Buckingham Palace, an honour which is very, very rarely accorded to party political agents. It showed how much their work had been appreciated at 10 Downing Street.

The local party workers, those who had supported, and, with very few exceptions, those who had opposed my nomination, threw themselves into the campaign with total loyalty. The agent set my wife and me a really punishing schedule; and we had to prove that we could stand up to it. It was something of an endurance test; but I think that we passed it satisfactorily; and we seemed to earn the respect, sometimes even the affection, of many party workers in Colwyn Bay; in

Rhyl of course we were, as always, almost entirely surrounded by friends.

I knew how desperately important it was going to be to develop these personal friendships with our party workers; for there was no doubt that their views and mine were widely different on a large and growing number of issues. The price of liberty, for an independent-minded MP, is eternal coffee mornings.

It was not only our own party workers that my wife and I set out to win over. We wanted to get as deeply involved as we could in the life of the town, and to develop close relations with active people of all political beliefs. It seemed to me that, even if my views put a strain on the loyalty of some party workers, they might be deterred from moving against me if they thought that I commanded widespread support throughout the town.

It did not take us long to get involved with organisations such as Pensioners Voice, the local branches of charities such as Amnesty, the Red Cross, UNICEF, the Hospital League of Friends, the churches of all denominations and all the schools including the three independent schools in Colwyn Bay. Anyone who has had to do this business of 'nursing' a constituency will know how time-consuming, but also how rewarding, it can be.

Within a couple of years we had formed many real friendships in the Colwyn end of the constituency; as we had already done at the Rhyl end. The clergy were particularly helpful and friendly to us in this matter. The Vicar of Rhyl, Canon Herbert Lloyd, had long been a very special friend and support; and there were many occasions when I was perplexed and turned to him for wise counsel and for comfort. He is a man of infinite humour and uncomplicated goodness; to go to a service in his handsome Victorian church, St Thomas's, is to rediscover what joyous fun religious practice can be. When my wife and I felt a bit down we would treat ourselves to St Thomas's. To watch the seemingly endless procession of elderly, infirm, and often mentally handicapped worshippers being helped down the chancel steps after taking Holy Communion was like having a ringside seat at the Pool of Bethesda. One of the happiest occasions in the year was the annual Rogation Day service, when Herbert Lloyd would bless the fishing boats as they left the harbour on the rising evening tide; and the waters crept ever closer to his feet as the last verses of 'For those in peril on the sea' drew to their close.

One incident has passed into the folklore of Rhyl. The vicar and I with our wives were attending a concert in the nearby church of St John's. At the interval I said to Herbert Lloyd, 'I think I'm just going to pop out and spend a penny'. 'Well, there's nowhere hereabouts', said he, 'but you might try the Naval Club next door. And, since you are going I think I'll go too'. So, telling our wives we would be back in a minute we dashed across the road to the Naval Club. As we entered the doors we found the Club President, all the Committee, the Mayor and Mayoress drawn up in a line; it was their gala night. 'What a nice surprise; the Vicar and the Member come specially to join us'; and so, before we could fulfil the primary purpose of our visit ('We've just dropped in to pay our water rates', said Herbert) we had to do the round of the club, being stood drinks by everybody, and returning somewhat the worse for wear to our by now very anxious wives nearly half an hour later.

I needed to cement such friendships, for there was no doubt that my independent stand on many issues did impose a strain on the loyalty of some of my more orthodox-minded supporters.

I had no hesitation in giving support to the Government, in

particular to the Secretary of State for Energy, Peter Walker, in the year-long battle against Arthur Scargill's coal strike. This seemed to me a rerun of the 1974 attempt by one union to impose its will on the elected Government; except that, instead of the weak moderate, Joe Gormley, at the head of the strike there was the openly insurrectionist Arthur Scargill. But even in this affair I seem to have upset some of my supporters by saying that, while I could see no merit in Scargill at all, I had to concede a certain nobility in the solidarity which the miners of South Wales, whose pits were not at that stage threatened with closure, were showing in support of miners in other areas; and I suggested that there might be something we could all learn from this display of solidarity. There was one other incident which gave offence. During the bitterest period of the dispute a young striking miner dropped a lump of concrete off a motorway bridge on to a taxi which was carrying a working miner to his pit; and the taxi-driver was killed. It was an act of brutal thuggishness, and the criminal got, and deserved, a long prison sentence. But it was *not* murder; and it was of murder that he was convicted. His local MP, Ted Rowlands, sought my support against the murder accusation, and I felt bound to give it, for it was patently obvious that there had been no intention to cause the death of even the working miner, let alone the taxi-driver. When passions are running as high as they were then my willingness to concede that there might be mitigating circumstances was regarded by some as tantamount to condoning the crime itself.

There was another incident which raised some eyebrows. A young RAF aircraftsman in my constituency was one of a group of seven servicemen stationed at GCHQ in Cyprus who were accused of passing secret information to an enemy. Lord Cledwyn of Penrhos, Labour leader in the Lords, and formerly MP for Anglesey, and for whom I have a high regard, asked me to look into this case, because he knew the boy's family, and vouched for their worth. I did look into the case; and became convinced that the evidence against at any rate some of the accused, and certainly that against my constituent, was insufficient to give any serious prospect of getting a conviction; and that in any case it was quite inadmissible to hold young servicemen of hitherto unblemished character in prison for the greater part of a year while the case against them was being prepared. Having failed to get my man let out on bail from Wormwood Scrubs, where I was horrified to find him, I made a public protest to Michael Heseltine, then the Secretary of State for Defence. I warned him that he stood no chance of getting a conviction, and that if he continued to oppose bail for these servicemen he would face the need for a humiliating apology and for compensation. The fact that I was proved right shortly afterwards did nothing to enhance my reputation as a defender of everything done by the Government.

In 1983 Mr Speaker Thomas retired, and was succeeded by Mr Speaker Weatherill. George Thomas had been Speaker since 1976 and was the first Labour occupant of the Chair. On coming to power in 1979 Mrs Thatcher might have been expected to replace him with a Tory MP; that would have accorded with most precedents. But she had reason to suppose that George Thomas would prove a positive asset to her as Speaker, and she was right. He was one of her most valuable and reliable allies.

George Thomas, with his unique gift for defusing the rows which blow up so readily in the Commons, his inimitable humour, and his real authority, was clearly going to be a hard act to follow. I remember one occasion when Dr Ian Paisley had decided that he would put on a major demo to draw attention to his anger over developments in Northern Ireland. Although the Chamber was not crowded, he chose to sit, not in his usual seat on the Government side of the House, but in one of the upstairs overflow galleries reserved for MPs. The Secretary of State for Northern Ireland was at the Despatch Box, making a statement about Northern Ireland. Paisley kept up a running barrage of insults, repeatedly calling him a traitor. The Speaker called him to order. Paisley went on yelling. Mr Speaker ordered him to sit down. The yelling continued. Mr Speaker then 'named' him. This is the ultimate deterrent; a Member who is named is thereby suspended for five days. But Paisley took no notice. Now Mr Speaker had to play his last card. He ordered the Serjeant at Arms to escort Mr Paisley from the Chamber. The Serjeant, who is the only person in the House who still wears his sword in the Chamber (the rest of us have loops of red tape on which to hang our swords as we arrive in the Members' cloakroom), on the rare occasions when he has to carry out the duty of escorting a Member from the Chamber, normally walks up to him, bows to him, and then walks out with him. This time, however, the Serjeant could not easily do that. He had first to leave the Chamber, disappear into the Members' lobby, go up the stairs, and appear though the door at the back of the upstairs gallery. Peter Thorne, the then Serjeant, was a gallant officer, but a man of slight build. Paisley is, of course, built like the Bull of Bashan. There was a moment when we expected to see the two men engage in combat at the edge of the gallery, like Sherlock Holmes and Professor Moriarty at the Reichenbach Falls, with one of them, probably the Serjeant, being hurled to his death below. And then, at the critical moment, with superlative timing, George Thomas struck: 'I warn the Honourable Gentleman that, if the Serjeant at Arms has but so much as to lay a finger on his sleeve, he will be suspended from the service of this House, not for five days, but for the remainder of this session'. And Paisley slunk out.

It is hard to imagine Mr Speaker Weatherill achieving a dramatic coup of this power. He is a Speaker in a very different mould. He had previously been Mrs Thatcher's Deputy Chief Whip; and the circumstances in which he lost that post are worth recounting. Early in 1979 the Commons had to vote on the method of election to the European Parliament for the elections to be held for that body in 1980. Every other Member country was going to use some system of proportional representation. But the Labour Government in Britain, while making plain its hostility to the idea of PR, nonetheless left this particular decision to a free vote. Jack Weatherill is a long-standing supporter of proportional representation (as am I); and, this being a free vote, he voted accordingly. As he came out of the voting lobby he encountered a pair of flashing blue eyes. 'Do you know what you have done?' 'Yes, I have just voted on a free vote for using PR for the European elections'. 'And do you know who you are?' 'Yes, I am your deputy chief whip'. 'No longer', she said.

So Jack Weatherill was exiled to the unrewarding post of Chairman of Ways and Means, in other words Deputy Speaker. During the next twelve months Jack made it his business to seek out and have a friendly chat with just about every single MP of every party. When the time came for George Thomas to retire to the Lords with his viscountcy, there was no doubt who would be the backbenchers' choice to succeed him.

It is the House of Commons, not the Government, which chooses the Speaker; but in practice the House usually endorses some figure who has been chosen by the Government and who is acceptable to the Opposition. Jack Weatherill was most certainly not Mrs Thatcher's choice for the post. Oddly enough she seems to have wanted Francis Pym, who had been dropped from the Foreign Office, but whose House of Commons skills had been demonstrated as Chief Whip, and as Leader of the House. But the House of Commons would have none of this. In those days Mrs Thatcher did not have the authority to defy the collective will of the House of Commons in a matter which was not even the proper concern of the Government; and Mr Speaker Weatherill was installed as the backbenchers' Speaker. And that he has been ever since. Mrs Thatcher did all she could to stop him getting the job; and, for some months after he got it, and at intervals ever since, her more zealous partisans in the Conservative Party have deliberately set out to destabilise him by making his task as difficult as possible, even to the extent of provoking disorderly scenes more appropriate to the football terraces of Leeds United.

Mr Speaker Weatherill may not have the natural authority or the histrionic gifts of Mr Speaker Thomas; but his fairness and impartiality are beyond dispute, and he enjoys the respect and admiration of backbench Members on both sides of the House.

At about this time I was invited to join a group of Tory MPs who were becoming increasingly concerned about some of the recent trends in Government policy. The group took the name of Centre Forward, and met about once a week under the chairmanship of Francis Pym. It was not a homogeneous group; there did not seem to be much common background or outlook among its members, other than a vague somewhat aristocratic distaste for certain aspects of Thatcherism. The whole operation was doomed from the outset; one or two Members who had joined without understanding what it was about were easily induced by the Whips to resign rather noisily, thus exposing the whole thing to some not entirely undeserved ridicule. It seemed to me to be a group which was willing to wound and yet afraid to strike. After all, had we been really serious in our purpose to influence Government policy we would, at the very least, have taken steps to ensure that there was a maximum turn-out of abstentions or hostile votes each time the Government did something particularly outrageous. But the very notion of such co-ordinated action sent shivers down the spines of the rather staid members of Centre Forward, and, after all, Francis Pym *had* been Chief Whip. For a Tory MP to vote against the Government might be condoned; but to organise others to do so was more what you might expect from shop stewards and their ilk; it is not the sort of thing that any decent Tory would do. So it was that when Michael Mates attempted to organise a backbench vote to make the poll tax ever so slightly less unjust, orders went out from Downing Street that he was to be ousted from every elected post which he held in the party; and the Praetorian Guard of the Party were ordered to ensure his defeat in every election for party office in which he stood.

All this may help to explain why revolts against the Government in this Parliament have been so conspicuously unsuccessful. The feeling is now widespread that any revolt is foredoomed to failure. That may be so. But it is surely no reason for not trying to organise opposition within the party to policies which show clear evidence of gross insensitivity to deeply held popular convictions. And that was what we round the table at Centre Forward were not prepared to do. We deserved to fail.

Even my keenest supporters in the constituency were none too pleased that I had joined Centre Forward; and I cannot claim that it was worth incurring their displeasure for so footling a cause.

At the end of 1986 a rather more serious issue arose. Michael Heseltine resigned from the Cabinet in protest at the leaking of a confidential letter to him from the Solicitor-General regarding the future of Westland helicopters; and there was some reason to suppose that the leak had been authorised by the Prime Minister herself. The ensuing crisis, which resulted also in the resignation of Leon Brittan, who had appeared to be in league with the Prime Minister in the plot against Heseltine, did immense damage to her credibility. There were many Conservative MPs who believed that her position was now impossible (particularly as regards the enquiry into responsibility for the leaking of the letter; for she herself *must* have known the truth which she instructed others to seek out, but which she refused to divulge to the enquiry). But I was the only Tory MP who went so far as to call for the Prime Minister to resign. I did not find much support for my stand, even among my colleagues of Centre Forward.

On 14 April 1986 American F111 fighter-bombers, flying from their British base, bombed Tripoli in Libya in retaliation for the alleged complicity of Libya's ruler, Colonel Gaddafi, in a terrorist bomb outrage in Beirut, in which US servicemen had been killed. The raid killed a few women and children, but did no more than frighten Gaddafi.

As the news of this operation began to come through, Tim Renton, then a junior Foreign Office minister, dashed around the corridors of the Commons, collecting as many Tory MPs as he could find in the middle of the morning for an emergency briefing on the matter. He explained how the Prime Minister had really had no option after the help which the Americans had given us over the Falklands, but to accede to the American request to use their British base for this operation, even though other Western governments had refused to allow the US sortie even to overfly their territory. The fifteen or so Conservative Members present were almost unanimous in their rejection of this argument; one very senior and rightly respected MP said that the Americans had behaved no better than the terrorists which they were supposed to be punishing, and that it was unacceptable for the British Government to condone such behaviour. In the division that night on a motion to approve the Prime Minister's action that same MP, like every other Tory, voted to approve her action; every MP but one. I was that one. It seemed to me then, and it still seems to me now, utterly unacceptable to use aerial bombing, which is certain to, and which did, kill innocent people, for the purpose of retaliation; and if a similar issue arises again I will vote the same way again.

My vote against the Government on the Libyan bombing was the most serious of many charges brought against me in an overheated meeting of the Executive Committee of the Clwyd North West Conservative Association on 27 June 1986. Libya, the miners' strike, my support for the airman from Cyprus, my conduct over Westland; it all added up to a catalogue of disloyalty to the Leader; against that my supporters argued the work which my wife and I had done in the constituency, and our undoubted popularity. The officers of the Association were wonderfully loyal; and we eventually carried the day by some 56 votes to 48, with about three abstentions. It was a close shave.

And so we came to the 1987 Election. I entered on that campaign with renewed determination to go on serving the interests of my constituents, with whom my links seemed to be getting ever closer; but with quite remarkably little enthusiasm for many of the items in the Party's manifesto. One thing I could unfeignedly rejoice in: the final destruction of trade union claims to usurp the governance of the country. This seemed to me an achievement so crucial as to compensate for many other things in the programme which I found unattractive. I was not even sure that it was wise to go very much further in hobbling the unions. I saw little advantage in privatising electricity, and none at all in privatising water, especially in Wales, where it is widely seen to have a special God-given quality.

But above all, I could see no sense, or justice or electoral advantage in the poll tax; and I had no hesitation in saying so. In fact I did all I could to keep politics out of my election address and out of my campaign, which I fought entirely on my record as an independent-minded MP at the service of his constituents. I don't suppose that had anything to do with it, but I did get a substantial increase in my majority, which was the largest Conservative majority in Wales.

The 1987 Election campaign was an exceptionally dull one; and in my own constituency it was a very low-key, good-tempered affair. I had good relations with my opponents, and, despite some of the recent differences, my wife and I worked very happily indeed with all our party workers, including those who had refused the hand of friendship which I had held out to them in the 1983 election. The seat was considered a safe one by Central Office, so that we were not much bothered by visits from Ministers, with one notable exception. Peter Walker, the Secretary of State for Energy, came for a midday walk-about and lunch. I was particularly glad to have him, as I had long regarded him as the doughtiest champion of traditional, One Nation Conservatism within the party and the Cabinet, apart from the high regard which I had for him personally. During his brief visit he threw himself into the campaign with his usual energy; including a visit to Abergele sheep market in which, with all the authority of a highly popular ex-Minister of Agriculture, he extolled my virtues as a constituency MP to a dutifully attentive group of Welsh sheep farmers who spoke little or no English and who came mainly from constituencies many miles away. Afterwards at lunch with him we speculated on who might be the next Secretary of State for Wales, for Nicholas Edwards had announced that he was retiring from the job and from the Commons. 'What about Norman Tebbit?' suggested Peter helpfully.

# CHAPTER TWELVE

# Walker's Wales

## 1987–1989

The announcement from 10 Downing Street that the new Secretary of State for Wales was to be Peter Walker was one of the most astonishing and most welcome pieces of news I have ever heard. I have given a good deal of thought to the matter, but I still cannot entirely satisfy myself as to the reasons why Mrs Thatcher offered him the job, still less why he accepted it. Be that as it may, the whole outlook was transformed as far as I was concerned. Whatever doubts I might have about the general trend of government policy, I could with a full heart support Peter Walker's action in Wales; for I knew that he would not hesitate to use the very considerable powers available to him in the Welsh Office to spread the Thatcher-induced prosperity far more widely throughout all areas and all income groups in Wales than the free play of market forces could possibly do. What I had not realised was how far Walker would succeed in carrying with him the local authorities, mostly Labour controlled, the trade unions, the various public bodies, all the Welsh press, and, with the exception of three or four incurably sourpuss Labour MPs, pretty well every Welsh MP of every party.

It was not just Peter Walker's action in Wales that I could enthusiastically support. For at any rate the first two years in his new post, Walker not merely continued but intensified his thinly veiled criticism of the Prime Minister's style and policies, and set out the need for the Conservative Party to demonstrate its concern for the less successful in our society and the less favoured regions of the UK. Furthermore, he made it perfectly plain that he was not prepared to stay in the job if he was not given the means to do it properly; and he carried on a series of highly publicised battles with the Treasury at each annual public expenditure round so as to ensure that Wales got far more than its fair share of public expenditure. On top of that, he secured for Wales a totally disproportionate share in inward investment largely from Japan, but also from the US and from other EC countries. It was a major success story; and it did not go unnoticed in England, where it excited some jealousy among Conservative MPs whose constituencies were not getting the same kind of favours. What some of the more doctrinaire among them pointed out with glee was that Walker's economic policies and his personal popularity were not actually achieving much by way of electoral success for the Tories in Wales. Their curmudgeonly attitude seemed to get some endorsement when, after the sad death of my very dear friend Raymond Gower, his seat in the Vale of Glamorgan, a seat which he had turned from being highly marginal into a safe Conversative one by his tireless work on behalf of all his constituents, was won by Labour in a highly publicised by-election. My wife and I worked very hard to support the Conservative candidate in that by-election. We were struck by the huge personal following which Raymond Gower had enjoyed, and by the damage which had been done to the Conservative cause in the area by the narrow-minded, quarrelsome local Conservative Association which had been notably disloyal to Raymond in recent years.

I was privileged to be invited to deliver the address for Raymond's memorial services, both to a crowded congregation in his own church in Cardiff, and to a smaller congregation, with the Prime Minister and the Speaker sitting in the front row of the crypt chapel at Westminster. On both occasions I spoke of Raymond's selfless loyalty to the Conservative party, but also of his devotion to a gentler, more unselfish kind of Conservatism than was in fashion today. I had the impression that my words were going down rather better with the Speaker than they were with the Prime Minister.

A gentler, more unselfish kind of Conservatism. I had used the words to describe Raymond Gower's outlook. But I could take it to myself also. I was finding something increasingly unattractive not only about the Prime Minister's style, but also about her policies, which were now the authorised version of Conservatism.

I acknowledge her achievement, back in 1979, in making Britain, formerly at the mercy of trade union abuse of power, once again governable – though it has to be said that the rise in unemployment which followed the 1981 Budget had something to do with the loss of trade union power. I acknowledge also the growth in national wealth creation, part of which does come from the release of energies previously pent up by excessive taxation and regulation; but it has to be said that the revenue from North Sea oil had something to do with that. There has been a large increase in real terms in personal incomes; there has been an increase also in public provision for the social services and the environment; but has it kept pace with the growth in personal living standards?

The inescapable fact is that standards of education, public transport, state schools, both as regard buildings and staffing, hospitals, street cleaning, policing, all are less good than they should be, and often downright unacceptable. Those who are primarily dependent on state benefits – retired pensioners without a second pension, the long-term sick, single parents – are expected to subsist on an income which is barely sufficient to support a reasonable level of personal dignity, and leaves no margin at all for emergencies. And when the emergencies occur, they are expected to borrow from the Social Fund (if that has not run out for the year), and then to repay the debt out of an income which is already below subsistence level.

The plight of those only slightly less poor, with savings of £8,000 or so (hardly great riches today), is almost more pitiable, for they lose all entitlement to the means-tested benefits which the Government has multiplied in the process of what is glibly called 'targetting benefits to those in greatest need'.

Part of the trouble arises from the instructions given to Norman Fowler when he was Secretary of State for Health and Social Services in 1985 to conduct a review of the social security system, and produce new proposals within six months. Three busy Ministers were to work out in six months what a Royal Commission would have needed two years for. It is surprising that the results were not even more unsatisfactory than they were; for the Ministers were not allowed to take into consideration the effect of tax policies (under which people pay the full standard rate of tax on even the lowest slice of taxable income; and that is low indeed), nor the cost of fuel, transport, telephone, TV licence, rates (or poll tax) of which even the poorest are now expected to pay 20 per cent.

Such care to avoid any excessive generosity to the poorest and near poor might have been tolerable if we were all in the same boat together. But for many millions this is a time of lavish and ostentatious prosperity. I don't want to see equality; it is a deadening doctrine. But I think that there should be some limits to inequality, even if they are very wide ones; and I find it hard to stomach still further moves towards widening the gap between rich and poor.

It is the Government's claim to have kept at arm's length from the economy wherever possible, and to keep out of the business of redistribution, which should trickle beneficently down from the process of wealth creation unleashed by deregulation. Frankly I think this is nonsense; but it is not even true that it is the Government's policy. The most blatant example of the tax system favouring the better off is mortgage interest relief, which even in these days of crippling interest rates confers substantial tax advantages on those who anyway possess a steadily appreciating capital asset. This is the most indefensible of tax policies in a nation which is already spending quite enough of its resources on housing; and the principal effect is to push up the price of houses. Nigel Lawson wanted to phase it out; but Mrs Thatcher has made it plain that she will never allow any reduction in this tax benefit to those who need it least.

Recent changes to permit the separate taxation of husbands and wives may make good economic sense; but it is another tax concession to those in lesser need.

And then there are the tax advantages enjoyed by pension funds. This is a prickly nettle which only Michael Heseltine has had the courage to grasp; for it is one of the factors which enables the Government to boast that the average incomes of pensioners have increased substantially. But it is a concession which is both socially and economically contestable, and which helps to suck resources away from the regions and towards the purely money-making activities of the City of London.

And there is the monstrous poll tax; a major tax concession to those who can afford to live in valuable homes in salubrious areas, and a heavy burden on those who can afford only cheap accommodation or who live in an area of social deprivation.

All this amounts to concentrating help on those who need it least; and it is being done by a Government which keeps talking about targetting benefits on the neediest.

The Ministers in the departments with primary responsibility for ensuring some elements of social fairness, the DSS and the Department of Health, are doing their best with the limited money they are allowed. But in order to provide any protection for the very weakest, they have had to resort more and more to the process of targetting benefits to the neediest which other arms of government are so busily reversing, and which anyway penalises the thrifty or the provident.

And then there is the problem of young people who have excluded themselves from benefit, many of them sleeping rough on the pavements of our big cities, or begging. Many of them have only themselves to blame for their plight, and it may comfort the smug to reflect on this; but it does not remove the unattractive and pitiable spectacle. There are others who have been forced by circumstances entirely beyond their control into a situation where they are excluded from all state benefits.

I know, from my knowledge of history, that the elimination of poverty is a pipe dream, and that no satisfactory solution has ever been found in any country. But I cannot avoid the feeling that for the poorest in our society, the very old, some of the young, the chronic sick, things are getting slowly but steadily worse as the affluence of the large majority equally steadily increases.

Much of the trouble lies in the Government's ambivalent attitude towards public spending. For her first few years in office Mrs Thatcher never ceased to boast of the cuts she was making in public expenditure. Now there has been a change in attitude by most Ministers. For Mrs Thatcher herself all public expenditure, except on defence, is money filched from the taxpayer's pocket and lavishly spent by some public body like a drunken sailor. During the past few years, as the public attitude has shifted, other Ministers regularly, and even Mrs Thatcher fitfully, try to give the opposite impression; that they are actually increasing public expenditure on such things as health, training, public transport, help for the disabled. These claims are perfectly valid but they convey a confusing picture. A very middle-of-the-road Tory who was sitting next to me at Question Time when some Minister was telling us of his Department's increased expenditure on some worthy objective asked me, 'Is he admitting it, or boasting about it?'

All in all, I was finding by mid-1989 that the Government, in pursuit of its ideologically motivated objectives, was losing sight of that precious concept of balance which should at all times be present in our national life. The rich were too rich, the poor too poor, and the Government, having destroyed the trade unions and emasculated local government, had, for all its claims to be engaged in a process of decentralising power, become altogether too powerful for the good health of our nation.

# CHAPTER THIRTEEN

# The European Fiasco

## January–June 1989

The five-yearly election for the European Parliament took place in June 1989. Back in 1984, within a few months of my keenly fought contest with Miss Beata Brookes for the Clwyd North West nomination, I had not merely proposed her as the candidate for the North Wales Euro-seat, but, almost alone among Conservative MPs, campaigned vigorously for her in that year's Euro-election. Again, in 1989, I and my wife were no less assiduous in our support; and we ranged widely through my constituency and in neighbouring ones urging the voters to turn out for her to reward her for the tremendous work she had done for the people of North Wales in the preceding ten years.

Throughout this book I have made it clear that I am deeply unhappy about Mrs Thatcher's attitude towards foreign affairs; primarily, but not solely, her attitude towards the European Community.

It is now part of holy writ in Conservative circles that Mrs Thatcher has been a doughty and successful defender of

Britain's interests in the world. It is certainly true that in the Falklands operation she demonstrated that it was dangerous to twist the lion's tail; and she deserves all credit for the courage and resolution which she showed in sending the navy to do battle 8,000 miles away with no air cover. In honesty I have also to add that the one country where her name is sincerely blessed is Argentina, as I found for myself when I visited Buenos Aires a few months after the conflict, and found that for most Argentinians the pain of losing the Falklands was drowned in joy at getting rid of the repressive Junta.

But Falklands apart (and there would have been no need for that operation if the Government had not funked the task of getting the Commons and the Islanders to swallow a sensible working relationship with Argentina), Mrs Thatcher's incursions into foreign affairs have on the whole been less successful than she has taken credit for – and sometimes spectacularly so.

She began as she meant to go on. Before the 1979 election, when she was touring Australia as Leader of the Opposition, she came out in support of Ian Smith's illegal white minority government in Rhodesia; and it took all the toughness and skill of Lord Carrington to rescue her from that gaffe, and to negotiate a peaceful handover of power to a properly elected government in Zimbabwe.

What she usually claims, and is rightly given credit for, is a large reduction in the size of Britain's contribution to the budget of the European Community. This undoubtedly is a real achievement; but the price for it was a serious loss of Britain's ability to secure other, more permanent and more crucial changes in EC policy. Because of Mrs Thatcher's insistence on 'getting our money back', she alienated those other members of the Community who might have been prepared to support us on other issues. She also contributed to making the EC less popular among people in this country, which was an unwise thing to do since even she admits that Britain has no choice but to belong to the EC – so what is achieved by making it unpopular? She opposed the idea of the Single European Act, which provides for majority voting on certain issues; but even she admits that it would not have been possible to make progress towards the elimination of barriers to trade (the single market) without the Single European Act.

It is not that her policy towards the EC is wrong so much as that it does not make sense. She will not allow the Conservative MEPs in the European Parliament room for manoeuvre, which they must have if they are to form alliances with other right-wing groups in that Parliament so as to foward British interests there. On the contrary, they have been told that it is their job to stick to the party line at whatever cost.

The end result of her much trumpeted 'Batting for Britain' in Europe is that we now find ourselves increasingly excluded from the central decision-making process in the European Community, the one outcome above all others which we sought to avoid when, in 1962, Harold Macmillan rightly concluded that Britain's vital national interests required that we get into the EEC, and right in. The first tangible result of this exclusion is likely to be the gradual transfer of the Community's financial centre from the City of London to Frankfurt, in consequence not only of our tardiness in joining the Exchange Rate Mechanism of the European Monetary System, or even of our opposition to further advances towards European Monetary Union and the other elements in the Delors Plan, but still more because of Mrs Thatcher's foot-dragging approach to all schemes of European integration.

Time and time again, the effect of her policy has been to isolate Britain. I believe that over South African sanctions she had more right on her side than those who were clamouring for sanctions to be imposed or retained. However, by allowing herself to be isolated on this issue, as she was so spectacularly at the Kuala Lumpur Commonwealth Conference ('If I am one against forty-seven I feel sorry for the forty-seven'), she contrived to send entirely the wrong signal to the remaining supporters of apartheid in South Africa, and she conveyed the impression that she hates apartheid a little, and sanctions a lot.

She is always looking over her shoulder at the electorate and, in the field of foreign affairs at least, is all too ready to pander to people's sillier prejudices. One of the reasons why she is so deeply distrustful of the Foreign Office is precisely because that Department takes little or no account of British electoral considerations. When she went to China in 1982 she tried to bully the Chinese over Hong Kong, and she got a good press back home for her robust championship of British interests. In consequence the Chinese lost face; and thereafter were far less ready to make concessions over the future of the colony. The wretched Foreign Secretary was left to pick up the pieces; and it was he who got the blame for the very unsatisfactory result.

The Prime Minister is no doubt echoing public anxiety when she voices her disquiet over German reunification. But what can she hope to achieve by publicly voicing it? Reunification is going ahead anyway, and it is not just wise to make the best of it; it is folly to do otherwise.

Even on defence policy, which has been her strongest suit throughout, she is now not only isolated but absurd. It can make no conceivable sense to press ahead as she still apparently wants with the modernisation of NATO's tactical nuclear weapons; who on earth now wants to target short-range missiles on Prague or Leipzig?

She may be on stronger ground electorally in clinging to the British independent nuclear deterrent; although it has to be said that the strategic arguments for this 1950s concept are looking decidedly threadbare. But, whatever the electorate may say, history will be very unforgiving if, by clinging to Britain's ageing strategic deterrent, she damages the chances of an international agreement on security at a much lower level of armaments. I believe that the argument for retaining some degree of nuclear deterrence is still valid; but I can see no justification for updating it at vast expense and at some risk to the chances of all-round disarmament.

I have also confessed to being a believer in federalism. I should explain my own attitude towards Britain's relations with the rest of Europe, and how far I believe that federalism is relevant to these issues.

I have been an enthusiastic supporter of full British participation in the process of European integration since my involvement in the abortive negotiations for the European Defence Community in 1952. Of course, support for the process of integration and for British participation in that process do not necessarily go together; one of my most revered chiefs at the Foreign Office in the 1960s believed that the European Community was the best thing that had happened in Europe since the break-up of the Roman Empire; but he did not want Britain to join because he feared we would damage it. I hope that he will be proved wrong, and I intend to do all I can to prove him wrong.

The European Community is not a federation; and it would not become one even if all Monsieur Jacques Delors' proposals for economic union were to be adopted. It is a novel creature in world history; and rather than try to find one word to describe it, it might be better to follow the wise precept which Sir Alec Douglas Home laid down when he was Foreign

Secretary in 1970; that the European Community should be allowed by its member governments to evolve the institutions and fit them into the framework which would best enable it to carry out its purpose.

There are, it seems to me, two Community institutions which mark it out from any previous alliance or coalition of nations. The first, and the more conventional, is the Court of the European Communities at Luxembourg (to be distinguished from the International Court of Justice at the Hague, and the European Court of Human Rights at Strasbourg, neither of which has any connection with the European Community). What is special about the Community's Court is neither its genuinely international composition, nor the powers attributed to it to settle disputes between member states or points of Community law, but the quite special authority which it has now acquired through the almost invariable submission of even the most recalcitrant member states to its judgements. It is now unthinkable for any member to defy its ruling for long.

The other, and more original institution is the European Commission. Considering that the supranational Commission consists of national politicians many of whom retain purely national political ambitions, it is astonishing how far the Commission has managed over more than thirty years to retain its supranational corporate character, and how readily the great majority of Commissioners have set aside their purely national outlooks in order to carry out their tasks on behalf of the Community as a whole. But the key element in the Commission's role is not so much its composition as the function which it has been given to perform, and which more than anything else recalls the vision of Jean Monnet. The Commission is not, as is sometimes supposed, a mere international secretariat; it alone has the power to propose community legislation or joint community policies; it is then for the Council of Ministers to accept or reject these proposals, or for the European Parliament to seek to amend them.

The idea behind this is that the supranational Commission would be able to evolve policies and to frame legislation more forward-looking and of greater benefit to the Community as a whole than would ever have emerged from a process of horse-trading among the member governments in the Council of Ministers, where there would always have been one or more members looking fearfully over its shoulder at the looming electors, and afraid to commit itself.

This is one of those instances where the theoreticians have proved to be far more practical than the working politicians. The latter, beginning with de Gaulle, have sought to emascu-late the Commission, and to reduce it to little more than a secretariat. In so doing they managed to reduce the whole Community to impotence; and it is only in recent years that the Community has resumed some forward impetus; though not so much by allowing the Commission to resume its rightful role, as by making increased use of majority voting in the Council of Ministers.

Nonetheless it is the Commission and the Court which, even more than the directly elected European Parliament, give the Community its strength and its cohesion. Both are vulnerable to the same virus, that of unrestrained nationalism. Of course that ultimate right can never be totally extinguished, even though it is no longer practicable for member states of the EC to go to war with one another. But nationalism is a Franken-stein monster; and those who breathe life into his nostrils incur an awesome responsibility, as events in Soviet Central Asia demonstrate only too clearly.

I do not believe that civilised men and women should allow this monster to roam unchained. That is why I am a federalist, why I believe that nations should submit, voluntarily but as irrevocably as possible, to certain enforceable rules of conduct.

There is probably no word, except perhaps the word democracy, which is so widely misused as the word federalism. In the European context it is often taken to mean a United States of Europe in which the former nations would have no more a separate identity than Texas or Nebraska. Nothing could be further from the truth. In a federal Europe each nation would preserve its national character, its national way of doing things, its language, its criminal law, its press, radio and television. Only in those areas where it was absolutely indispensable would decisions be taken at the federal level. In Europe today such decisions would need to be taken at the European level in defence, protection of the environment, relations with countries outside the EC, and in such areas of economic policy as are necessary to enable the Community to function efficiently as a common market, an effective force in world economic development, while safeguarding the social welfare of its people. France would still be France, Spain would still be Spain, Britain would still be Britain. As a matter of fact it would also become rather easier for Wales to be Wales, Scotland to be Scotland, Corsica to be Corsica, Brittany to be Brittany and Catalonia to be Catalonia, without imperilling the fundamental integrity of Britain, France or Spain. To ram the point home, it should be understood once and for all that a federal state is the exact opposite of a unitary state where all decisions are taken at the centre.

Mrs Thatcher chooses to describe progress towards integration among the other eleven member states of the Community as an advance towards federalism. It isn't; and federalism is not what she says it is anyway. But the confusion makes it easier for her to parade her manifest reluctance to allow the European Community to attract loyalties which might detract in any way from purely national loyalties. In her famous Bruges speech in September 1988 she sought to roll back the frontiers of integration in Europe as she had rolled back the frontiers of socialism in Britain. Moreover, she reinforced her attack on integration by making a connexion between integration and socialism. There is no such connexion. The fact is that some of the European governments which are keenest on integration are more strongly and more consistently attached to free enterprise capitalism than she is. Nor is it true that there is fatal inconsistency between integration and national indentity. Just try to convince the French of that. There is no people on earth more passionately attached to their own, highly idiosyncratic way of life, nor more ready to talk the language or think the thoughts of integration.

Mrs Thatcher has also chosen to lump together progress towards European integration with socialism and bureaucracy. As she sees it, she has rid this country of socialism, and she has no intention of allowing a lot of European bureaucrats to push it in through the back door. In particular she has a violent aversion to the European Social Charter; and has made it plain that she regards it as a Marxist document and that she will have nothing to do with it.

It has to be said that in her outright opposition to the Social Charter Mrs Thatcher enjoys a degree of support from the Conservative Party and from British business and industry, which she does not have for her no less vehement opposition to British membership of the Exchange Rate Mechanism of the European Monetary System. And yet there is much in the Social Charter which derives directly from the Toryism of Lord Shaftesbury and Disraeli. And, unless the Tory Party is now to be regarded merely as a spokesman for management, there is surely some merit in the notion that workers in an enterprise should be given some say in what is to happen to that enterprise in the future. The take-over of a firm by some rapacious conglomerate is surely of as much concern to its workers as it is to the shareholders. I can see that it is difficult for us to go all the way with the notion of workers on the board which was inherent in the earlier drafts of the Social Charter; but it would be perfectly easy to devise schemes which would be compatible with British traditions of industrial relations, but which could nonetheless be fitted into the general framework of the Social Charter.

Moreover the Social Charter is one of the elements in the European Community which will make it easier for the countries of eastern Europe to draw closer.

Mrs Thatcher is right to insist that the arguments for integration in Western Europe must be looked at anew in the light of the wonderful things which are happening in Central and Eastern Europe. At first sight the re-emergence of the nations of Eastern Europe from their long suffocation in the arms of the Soviet bear, and the seeming break-up of the Soviet Union itself into its component nationalities, seem to justify Mrs Thatcher's view of nationalism as the force which cannot and should not be resisted and which will sweep away all fancy notions of integration, pooling of sovereignty, and rules and regulations imposed by faceless bureaucrats in Brussels.

But for those with any feel for history, the events in Eastern Europe carry as much menace as hope. In 1848, which offers an uncannily close parallel to the events of today, the nations of central Europe threw off the yoke of Austrian Imperialist rule; and at a later stage the nations of south-east Europe threw off the Turkish yoke. Nationalism and the love of liberty combined to defeat the tyrant's power; but it was nationalism which quickly became top dog, and remained there. Not that there is any necessary connexion between the love of freedom and the love of peace; revolutionary France was far more bellicose than royalist France had ever been. And it is as well to remember that most wars have been extremely popular, at any rate in their early stages.

It was not long before the newly emergent nations of Eastern Europe in the nineteenth century were at each other's throats, and before long dragging the bigger nations, who were their protectors, into the bloody, fratricidal conflict. It is a thoroughly alarming prospect; and though statesmanship must welcome it and make the best of it, it is most unwise to welcome it merely because it represents a disaster for socialism and the triumph of nationalism.

Of course it is futile to try to put the clock back; and it would be not just futile but wrong to try to restore Soviet influence over its former satellites. It may not be futile, but it is surely wrong to over-excite the nationalist feelings of the peoples of Eastern Europe.

The more percipient leaders of Eastern Europe are well aware of these dangers. Vaclav Havel, President of Czechoslovakia, is already urging some measure of integration between Czechoslovakia, Poland and Hungary. Nor are they all as ready as our more doctrinaire home-grown free-marketeers would have us believe to throw out all the babies of collective effort with the bathwater of state socialism. They value their welfare provision, the schools, hospitals and holiday camps; and they would like, if possible, to find a half-way house between socialism and the free-market economics of capitalism. It may not be possible to find one; but we in the West should take some account of their lingering attachment to welfare economics.

All of this suggests that it is nowhere near enough to rejoice in the proof that socialism does not work and that nationalism is indestructible. Just as the European Community, which has permanently reconciled age-old enemies in Western Europe, has offered a beacon of hope and a pole of attraction for the peoples of Eastern Europe; so now it offers them an eventual home and an immediate pattern for living together in harmony. It is, moreover, the only framework in which a reunited Germany can happily be contained; and it could even help to resolve the pressing problems created by the break-up of the Soviet Empire.

Back in 1950, Mrs Thatcher's great hero, Winston Churchill, said, 'National Sovereignty is not inviolable, and may be resolutely diminished for the sake of all the men in all the lands finding their way home together'.

However, such ideas are a world apart from the thinking of the Prime Minister, who set the tone for the 1989 Conservative Euro-election campaign.

I have to say very frankly that the Conservative campaign in the 1989 Euro-election was a disgrace. In her speech at Bruges the previous September, the Prime Minister had exposed her deep distaste for the European Community which she regarded as a group of semi-Marxist bureaucrats seeking to steal our money and to foist socialism on us by backhand methods. The Party's Euro-campaign was inspired by this ignoble theme; and was crudely designed to exploit the average Englishman's dislike of foreigners, and his firmly held conviction that they are sure to swindle him. The widely displayed campaign poster expressed it well:

'Stay at Home on 15th June,
and You'll Live on a Diet of Brussels'.

Despite her tireless work during the campaign, and still more during all the years that she had served the electors of

North Wales, Miss Brookes lost her seat, not to the deserving Dafydd Elis Thomas, who had fought an intelligent and moderate campaign on behalf of Plaid Cymru, but to a Labour Party plodder who had hitherto shown no interest in Europe whatever.

The North Wales seat, the only seat in Wales held by the Conservatives, was rightly regarded as a key marginal; and the media were taking a close interest in the result. BBC 2's *Newsnight* had sent their cameras into Flint Leisure Centre, where the count was conducted. When it was known that Miss Brookes had been beaten, she herself, after publicly correcting the Returning Officer for some lapses in procedure, left the premises and could not be found. The *Newsnight* cameras were lined up to interview victors and vanquished. I was the only Conservative MP who had turned up at the count; there was no one else to turn to for a Conservative comment on what had happened. 'To what', I was asked, 'do you attribute the loss of this seat?' I did not hesitate, 'To Mrs Thatcher', I replied. I was able to go on to say that Miss Brookes was in no way to blame, that no one could have worked harder, and that her defeat was due almost entirely to the shameful, defeatist, and negative campaign which had been conducted by the Party nationally, and for which Mrs Thatcher herself was clearly responsible. It is true that formal responsibility lay at the door of that decent man Peter Brooke, the Party Chairman; but anyone who had studied the Prime Minister's attitude before and during the campaign could not be aware that it reflected her outlook with total fidelity.

My comment excited a good deal of attention from the media and from some of my party workers; and I was invited to repeat them and to amplify them on various programmes. I had no hesitation in doing so. I was convinced then, and am more than ever convinced now, that the Prime Minister's cheap appeal to the most unworthy instincts of the British people was not merely bad statesmanship, it was bad politics; and that it would quite soon prove as damaging to the Party as it certainly would be to the country's long-term interests.

# CHAPTER FOURTEEN

# No One
# Stood Up

## July–October 1989

Events now began to speed up. At the end of July 1989 the Prime Minister carried out a much more dramatic reshuffle of her Cabinet than had been expected, sacking her much-respected and strongly pro-European Foreign Secretary, Sir Geoffrey Howe (he was sent to the salt mine of the Privy Council Office), and replacing him with the delightful but totally unknown John Major. I was very angry about this move; but for once I kept my mouth more or less shut. I felt certain that the Prime Minister wanted to have a poodle in the Foreign Office; it remained to be seen whether, in John Major, she had got one.

The Conservative Party Conference at Blackpool in October was a dreamlike affair. Everyone knew that the Party was in trouble, and that Labour was pulling away from us in the opinion polls. But it was one of the most genuinely successful and enthusiastic conferences for many years; and I am bound to say that the Prime Minister's speech at the end was one of the best she has ever given. One phrase in particular stuck in my mind, when she was speaking of Kinnock's sudden conversion to the European Community after years of opposition, and to multilateral disarmament after life-long membership of CND: 'If he can give up so easily the ideas which he has held for a lifetime, how quickly will he discard those he has adopted for electoral purposes?' In that phrase she summed up for me the reasons why, despite all my doubts over present policies and the present style of government, I remain a Conservative.

Soon after the Party Conference at which Nigel Lawson, the Chancellor of the Exchequer, had received a standing ovation, which was rare indeed for him, reports began to multiply of a rift between the Chancellor and the Prime Minister's favourite, though part-time economic adviser, Professor Alan Walters. From many of the Prime Minister's comments on such matters as the exchange rate, it seemed that she was paying more attention to her adviser than to her supposedly 'unassailable' Chancellor. Such reports had been rife for some twelve months. Lawson's 1987 Budget had been hailed as one of the boldest for decades, and for a while he was the toast of the Party, the architect of our victory to come. But, barely a year later, he was being blamed for everything that was beginning to go wrong, and plenty of things were going wrong.

The trouble was, of course, that Lawson was not allowed to follow his own chosen policies. They might, or they might not, have been successful; what was certain was that the evident rift between the Chancellor and the Prime Minister was a guarantee of failure. The most acute problem was over exchange rate policy. Lawson wanted to get sterling into the Exchange Rate Mechanism of the European Monetary System, and so provide a stable exchange rate. This would not necessarily have enabled him to lower interest rates; but it would at least have ensured that high interest rates achieved their objective. Lawson had other aims. He wanted to taper off mortgage interest relief, a hugely expensive subsidy intended to help first-time home buyers whose actual effect is to push house prices much higher than they would otherwise be; and he wanted to complement his tax cuts with an attack on the innumerable tax perks which go mainly to the better off.

But Lawson was not allowed to get on with the job, any more than Geoffrey Howe at the Foreign Office was allowed to get on with his. At every turn the Chancellor and the Foreign Secretary found the Prime Minister barring the way and telling them what to do ('Go and find out what the children are doing and tell them to stop it').

Until the resignation of Nigel Lawson in November 1989, and the much quieter subsequent resignations of Norman Fowler and Peter Walker, the members of the Cabinet seemed content to allow Mrs Thatcher to walk all over them. No one stood up to be counted, until at last Lawson could bear it no longer. He delivered an ultimatum. Either Mrs Thatcher agree to phase out her adviser, Professor Walters, or she lose her Chancellor.

The Prime Minister took no notice. Lawson resigned. Mrs Thatcher promptly appointed John Major in his place after what has to be the shortest ever tenure at the Foreign Office, and Douglas Hurd achieved his lifelong ambition of being Foreign Secretary. The reshuffle was deftly carried out, unlike the botched job at the end of July, and Nigel Lawson, after one powerful but restrained resignation speech, retired from the political scene never to be heard of again, except to the extent that he can now be safely blamed for everything that went wrong in the 1980s as Lord Barber was blamed for everything that went wrong in the early 1970s. '*Les absents ont toujours tort*' as the French say.

But it seemed to me that the Lawson affair raised some deep

issues, and that it was not right to allow Lawson to be buried in a forest clearing late at night. One by one, any Minister who stood up against the Prime Minister's way of doing things was either sacked, or felt compelled to resign. What none of them were ever prepared to do was to join forces with other colleagues who were similarly threatened. I felt that someone should make a stand; and that at the very least the Conservative Party should take a conscious decision about whether it wanted to submit to a President, and to judge by her recent comments about her determination to 'go on and on', a President for life.

Not since Neville Chamberlain has there been a Prime Minister who treats the Cabinet with such contempt, or who has gathered the reins of power so completely into a single pair of hands. It is an open secret that there has been an overwhelming majority in Cabinet for at least two years in favour of Britain joining the Exchange Rate Mechanism of the European Monetary System; but the Prime Minister has found one pretext after another for not joining, and no one seriously believes that she will ever give her approval for a step which would, at the very least, have ensured that high interest rates produced the desired result of curbing inflation.

It is none too easy to have respect for the members of a Cabinet who are so eager to lie down and be walked over. After Nigel Lawson's resignation I was asked whether I thought the Prime Minister ought to take a woman into her Cabinet. The right answer would have been that it was time she took a man into it.

Another area in which Mrs Thatcher had no difficulty establishing her dominance was the House of Commons, which she bestrode like a colossus almost from the day she moved into 10 Downing Street.

Poor Michael Foot was obliterated by her; and his more

agile successor, Neil Kinnock, took nearly five years to shed his addiction to Welsh verbosity. Mrs Thatcher was invulnerable at the Despatch Box; she was lethal with the rapier, and she knew when to use the bludgeon instead. I only once heard her put down; that was by Jim Callaghan after he had retired to the backbenches. In the course of some post mortem discussion on the Falklands campaign, Mrs Thatcher taunted him with, 'The Right Honourable Gentleman would not have had the guts to send the Task Force', to which he quietly replied, 'I would not have had to'. In the past year or so Mrs Thatcher has greatly modified her manner at the Despatch Box, perhaps to avoid scaring the televiewers; the result is that it is she who appears long-winded and woolly, whereas Neil Kinnock has developed an altogether new incisiveness.

Her mastery of the Commons was undoubtedly a major factor in establishing her national authority; but her churlishness towards her political opponents in the Commons has also contributed towards the sourness which has been such a feature of public life during her period of office. It is idle to regret the kind of relationship which existed between the Prime Minister and the Leader of the Opposition, or to sigh over the days when Arthur Balfour and Herbert Asquith, having slated one another with quite as much ferocity and a good deal more wit than is heard today, used to don their top hats and cloaks at the end of the evening debate, and stroll arm in arm across St James's Park to Lancaster House to be received together by the Duchess of Sutherland at the top of the grand staircase. Such days are gone; but I cannot believe that our public life is in any way enriched by the manifest contempt which Mrs Thatcher feels for Neil Kinnock or the detestation which he so clearly feels towards her.

Just as she treats her Ministers with contempt (but not, I hasten to add, her staff, for whom she is, quite simply, wonderful), she treats her political adversaries as if they were scarcely human. I have never heard her respond with even a hint of warmth to the occasional tribute paid to her across the floor of the House. The trouble is that she cannot conceive of any intelligent, honest person holding opinions which differ from her own. If you disagree with her you are a fool or a knave – except for the very, very few who are prepared to face a blazing row with her, and defeat her in argument. The only Ministers who have ever done this and lived are Lord Carrington and Peter Walker.

Because of the size of her parliamentary majority Mrs Thatcher has been able to treat the Conservative Party in Parliament with nearly though not quite as much contempt as she treats her Cabinet. She has been helped in this by the Whips' Office. It has to be said that the quality of the Whips, including, especially including, successive Chief Whips, has been extremely high throughout her tenure of office.

It is important to understand how heavily the Parliamentary cards are stacked in the Government's, any government's, favour. In the first place, most MPs are so overloaded with work that they often do not have time to familiarise themselves even with the broad issues, let alone the detail, of the measures on which they are voting. A mere handful of members are able to attend the debate, usually those who are hoping to be able to speak in it. Only for highly controversial debates on issues such as capital punishment or abortion is the Chamber full for the whole proceedings. This means that MPs usually vote without having heard any of the arguments; and they often discover in which lobby to vote (i.e., whether to vote 'Aye' or 'No') only by asking the Whips who stand on duty at the entrance to the voting lobby.

The days are long past when the Chief Whip and his Office used parade ground methods to enforce discipline, though such methods were habitual when I was first elected in 1964. Nowadays methods are much more subtle.

It is sometimes said that the only sanction available to the Whips is the threat to withhold the annual invitation to the Royal Garden Party. But there are other similar, but more effective sanctions. Most MPs very much enjoy, and derive much value from, official foreign visits. The delegations for these visits are usually settled in the Whips' Office. Rather more significant are threats of loss of promotion for persistent rebels; though anyone who recalls the career of, say, Harold Macmillan, should be able to use such threats to lick some of the younger and more impressionable MPs into line; they certainly used such methods to induce a few resignations from Centre Forward.

But the most effective pressure operating on a Member is that which comes from his local party, composed overwhelmingly of unquestioning loyalists, who will almost invariably censure their Member if he steps too far out of line. Up to a point the Whips can activate this pressure by discreet communication with the chairman of a recalcitrant Member's local Association. This can backfire. Sometimes the chairman will resent any effort from Westminster to put pressure on him to put pressure in his turn on the Member. There is a story, for whose accuracy I cannot vouch, that my former colleague Geraint Morgan figured in just such an attempt by the Whips, this time to induce him to attend the Commons rather more frequently than was his wont; in reply the Chief Whip received a furious rejoinder telling him to mind his own business and enquiring why Mr Morgan's outstanding qualities had not resulted in a ministerial appointment.

The art of whipping is, of course, very different in a parliament where the Government has a majority of a hundred or more, from when the majority is twenty or less. With the present huge majority the Whips cannot keep their Members constantly on the knife edge of loyalty, with the threat that a lost vote could precipitate an election. What the Whips can now do is to allow a substantial fraction of the party a night off every week or so. The effect of this is to reduce the Government's majority from one hundred to seventy or so; ample margin for error. But, if a revolt is threatened, then all leave is cancelled. The result is that every time there is a revolt against the Government, its majority actually goes *up*, instead of down. This may be regarded by the Whips as a highly satisfactory outcome. I believe, on the contrary, that it is extremely dangerous. Revolts occur when backbench MPs sense that there is deep unhappiness in their constituencies over the Government's policies. If the only palpable result of such revolts is to increase the Government's majority, the impression will inevitably be given to the country that the Government has closed its ears to popular discontent. This must be damaging to the health of our parliamentary system.

The Whip's Office is in a position to effect overkill; and it has a wide range of weapons to enable a graduated response to be made to any perceived threat. This part of their job they carry out to perfection. But they have another job to do. It is for them to convey to the Party's leaders, and to the Leader herself, the feelings of backbench members. There is no reason to suppose that they do not carry out this part of the job with conscientiousness. I know that the Whip who is responsible for me goes to extraordinary lengths to ascertain my views; and, for my part, I always make sure that I give him due warning if I am going to abstain or to vote against the Government. As I say, the Whips certainly do this part of their job very well. But I find it almost impossible to believe that the Prime Minister takes much notice of the views of the Party conveyed to her in this way.

A very worrying consequence of this is that the Party has ceased in any way to mirror public feeling. The more unpopular the policy, the more grimly the Whips round up the absentees and the waverers to vote for it. The end result is that when the Government does something quite peculiarly unacceptable, such as when they proposed to nominate the Council which was to run London during the year between the abolition of the GLC and the elections to the London boroughs, the majority for this outrageous proposal was even larger than usual.

Almost worse in the long run has been the abuse of the House of Lords' powers of revision. Among the peers who normally attend the upper house, the Government normally has a comfortable majority, but nothing like the huge majority it has in the Commons. On a number of occasions there have been enough Tory dissidents in the Lords to make quite substantial amendments to Government bills when these changes seemed to be called for by common sense, or by a feeling for the deep instincts of the British people – which the unelected House of Lords sometimes comprehends better than some MPs, whose huge majorities can incline them to a certain arrogance. But when Mrs Thatcher became aware that a large number of the Tory working peers were irreconcilably opposed to the poll tax, in addition to the unanimity of opposition and crossbench peers, she gave orders that every backwoods peer capable of speech or motion should be dragged into the Lords to support the Government; and once again the Government had a record majority for the least acceptable proposal in recent memory. The Government won their victory; but the Lords' reputation as a Chamber willing to stand up to even a Conservative government has been irretrievably wrecked; and the arguments for retaining even a reformed House of Lords under a Labour Government have been gravely weakened.

# CHAPTER FIFTEEN

# Challenge

## November–December 1989

It has been the rule in the Conservative Party since 1965 that the leader of the Party must submit to an annual election by the Party in the Commons. It was this procedure which Mrs Thatcher herself invoked perfectly properly in 1975 to overthrow Mr Heath. Since that date the annual election had been a mere formality, though there had been some mutterings about invoking it in 1986 at the time of the Westland affair; indeed when I had called at that time for Mrs Thatcher's resignation, Mr George Gardiner, a member of her Praetorian Guard, had mockingly suggested that if I would put my name forward he would gladly be my proposer. Perhaps I should make haste to add that Mr Gardiner was *not* my proposer in 1989!

But it did seem to me after Lawson's resignation that the time was right to renew my call for a challenge to Mrs Thatcher this year. I made the call in front of television cameras, so it attracted some publicity. Events then moved very fast indeed. I was telephoned in my office at the House of Commons by Chris Moncrieff, the indefatigable Press Association correspondent: 'I see you are calling for the Prime Minister to be opposed at the annual election this year. Who should it be to oppose her?'

'I really don't know. You can think of three or four people who would do it admirably.'

'Yes, but if none of them will, would you?'

'Don't be absurd. It has got to be a serious candidate.'

'But if none of them are prepared to do it, would you?'

'Well, I suppose that if absolutely nobody better can be found someone will have to offer themselves up as a burnt offering, and it might then have to be me.'

Ten minutes later I came downstairs to the Members' lobby, to be surrounded by a sea of journalists. Was it true that I was standing against Mrs Thatcher?

After a moment of panic I realised that I would have to go through with it; and so began the 1989 leadership challenge. Like Lord Byron, I awoke one day and found myself famous; unlike Lord Byron I had no achievement to justify that fame.

What had brought me to the point of launching a challenge to the Prime Minister? I hope that the narrative so far will have provided some clues. There were many moments during the contest when I wondered what on earth I was doing, and half expected to wake up and find it was all a dream, perhaps a nightmare.

I had been coming more and more firmly to the conclusion, especially during the preceding six months, that Mrs Thatcher was no longer the leader most likely to lead the Party to victory at the next election. I still valued her achievements, the deliverance of parliamentary democracy from the stranglehold of trade union power, the containment of inflation, the restoration of respect for Britain abroad. But it was nonetheless legitimate to ask whether she was still the person best placed to safeguard these achievements. Indeed, it seemed to me extraordinary, in this year of 1989 when all over eastern Europe the former ruling parties were subjecting their leaders to election, that in Britain alone the idea of making use of the machinery expressly provided for the election of a leader should be considered almost treasonable.

It would, of course, have been frivolous to activate the machinery for a leadership election merely because the machinery existed. Nor would it have been sufficient justification to require that the Prime Minister's apparent intention to carry on for many years to come, and to carry on with scant regard for the views of her Cabinet or her party, should be formally endorsed rather than allowed by default. I would not have been justified in doing what I did unless I had the gravest reservations, not merely about her style of governing, or about her chances of success, but about her policies themselves.

There were specific reasons why her chances of victory at the next election were slight. Her apparent invincibility was based on three successive victories, in each of which she had secured a *smaller* share of the popular vote. The size of her victory in 1983, and in 1987, was due less to her strength than to the temporary emergence of the centre parties as a genuine third force, snatching any possibility of a win from the Labour Party. Moreover that party was, under Michael Foot's leadership, palpably unelectable in 1983; and in 1987 still a long way from having any credible policies.

The situation which will face the Conservative Party in 1991 or 1992 will be very different. We shall be facing something very close to a straight fight with Labour. What is more, it will be a Labour Party with very much more voter appeal than in 1983 or 1987. Mr Kinnock may not yet look much like a Prime Minister; but he has managed to marginalise his left wing; he has loosened the grip of the unions on the party machine; he has dropped the more unappealing policies of wholesale nationalisation and penal taxation; as well as the previously disastrous unilateral disarmament policy and the threat of withdrawal from the European Community.

With its shiny new, if untried, policies, and a talented team on its Front Bench, Labour begins to look electable for the first time in ten years.

Moreover, even if many of the Labour Party's policies are rather after the fashion of 'These are my principles; and if you don't like them I have some others which you might like better', they nonetheless do have genuine appeal to the voters; for they seem to be more closely in tune, not just with the temporary whims of the electorate, but with the deeper, settled feelings of the British people. It was beginning to look as if the tide which had carried Mrs Thatcher to victory in 1979, and which she had harnessed so skilfully, was now on the turn, and she no longer had the skill to turn with it.

In 1979 the country was becoming tired of socialism and the ever-increasing power of government, local and national; and it was disheartened by the evident reluctance of incoming Conservative governments to reverse the ratchet. People wanted to keep more of the money they had earned by their skills or industry; they wanted to see effort rewarded; they were fed up with having their money taken away from them and wastefully spent by public bodies. Mrs Thatcher duly cut taxes; and most people's standard of living rose.

But after ten years of this beneficent process the rich have become very much richer; the poor, and perhaps to a greater extent the near poor (those with enough savings or small pensions to debar them from means-tested benefits), have become not merely relatively, but actually, poorer. And not a few of those who have gained by these changes feel sufficiently uncomfortable about it to register their disapproval in the ballot box.

What is more, even the rich are now finding that they cannot buy the things they most want; clean air, swept streets, better schools and hospitals, punctual and safe trains, golden sands. They do not believe that these things can be provided for them other than through public expenditure; they say, and they may even mean, that they are prepared to pay somewhat higher taxes if that is necessary. And they sense, rightly, that Mrs Thatcher is so implacably hostile to all forms of public expenditure, except on defence, that she is unable even to comprehend this fundamental change the public wants.

One of Mrs Thatcher's trump cards has been her aggressive stance towards foreigners, especially Europeans. I made no secret of the fact that it was her manifest distaste for everything that emanates from Europe that finally decided me to launch my challenge. But, although my own enthusiasm for a united Europe may not be widely shared, I really do believe that Mrs Thatcher's antipathy to Europe is becoming an electoral liability. People look across the Channel, and they see cleaner streets, trains that run on time, more generous pensions, more modern schools, more self confidence. There are good things to be had from Europe, so why is Mrs Thatcher reluctant to let us have them?

And so, because I believed that Mrs Thatcher would be less likely to win the next election than another leader (preferably Michael Heseltine); because I believed that her social and economic policies were out of tune with the deep instincts of the British people; because I believed that her European policies were disastrous for Britain and for Europe; and because I believed that she intended to press on with these policies, taking ever less account of the doubts being expressed all around her, I decided to invoke the established procedure for the election of a

Party leader. If the Conservative Party really wanted these policies under a leader who was going to go on and on and on, let them at least stop and think and then vote on the matter. This might well be the last chance for them to do so.

After my initial moment of panic I decided to press on.

The press were very properly derisive. 'Sir Nobody' was daring to challenge the greatest leader of all time; and the *Sun* treated its readers to '10 Things They Didn't Know About Sir Nobody'. It was widely assumed by everybody that I was a stalking horse for a more serious candidate, whether a genuine contender for power like Michael Heseltine, or a substantial figure with no desire to assume the leadership for himself like Sir Ian Gilmour. I must make it absolutely clear that I had no contact, direct or indirect, with any of the possible claimants for the throne. There was no plot against Mrs Thatcher; indeed it has been one of my complaints throughout that those who oppose Mrs Thatcher's policies or style have never been prepared to join forces. It is true that I lived in the constant expectation that long before the closing day for nominations, which was 23 November, a more redoubtable challenger would have appeared on the scene.

In the meantime I was receiving saturation publicity in the press and on radio and television. I was only too well aware that my achievement and personal stature in no way matched up to the publicity I was getting; and if ever I was tempted to believe that I had any real right to be boring the public night after night like this my wife was on hand to bring me down to earth. I seem to have managed not to make too much of a fool of myself, mainly because I could never quite believe what was happening to me, and I declined to take myself too seriously.

But it was a time of great strain for me, and even more for my wife. We were followed everywhere by the press, some of whom showed more consideration than others. One young press photographer attached himself to us like a limpet. He was a photographer from *The Sunday Times* and, oddly enough, he had been born and brought up in my constituency. In fact, he accompanied us on one of our weekend visits there. For most of a week this young man, Ian Parry, followed me and my wife wherever we went. Every time I went into a television studio, there was Ian, lurking behind the cameras, clicking away with his. He followed me to St Stephen's Green, to the almost inaccessible basement of the Queen Elizabeth Conference Centre; on trains, buses, waiting for taxis, there was Ian, and sometimes his girlfriend Philippa. Does it sound obtrusive? Nothing could be further from the truth. He was our guide, companion and friend in times of joy and times of worry. Three weeks later he was killed, flying back from Romania with the first press pictures which had been taken of those splendid and heady days of freedom in Bucharest. It was a great honour to be invited by his family to give the address at his memorial service in St Bride's.

As the closing day for nominations approached it began to look as if there was not going to be a more credible challenger and that I would be left to face the music alone. Sir Ian Gilmour has since said that he would have been prepared to put his name in, but that he had eventually decided to leave it to me. I think that there were two considerations. I had received so much publicity, much of it quite favourable, and all this would be wasted if I were now to pull out. The second consideration is more subtle. As long as the only challenge came from me, there was no risk of comparisons with Mrs Thatcher; Tory MPs were being asked, in effect, 'did they, or didn't they want Mrs Thatcher to go on?' But if a more serious contender, such as Ian Gilmour, was put up, there would inevitably have been a direct comparison between him and Mrs Thatcher, to which there could have been only one possible answer.

Now that it was clear that mine was the only name to be put forward, and that I was serious in my intention, pressure began to persuade me to desist. I am sorry to disappoint those who like the conspiracy theory but I have to report that there was absolutely no attempt at anything approaching arm-twisting or bullying. The Chairman of the 1922 Committee, Cranley Onslow, asked me to call on him, and asked me very courteously to desist. The Chief Whip, Tim Renton, asked me to call 'at my convenience'. I went to see him straight away. We had a most friendly conversation, with him doing his best to get me to change my mind; but once it became clear that I was not going to, we discussed over a cup of tea how the contest could be handled so as to do the minimum of damage to the Party. And certainly, if the Prime Minister wanted to minimise damage, she could not have done better than to appoint George Younger to conduct her campaign for her.

I kept no diary of events during the two weeks that the election 'campaign' lasted. There would not have been time to do so. Most days started with *Breakfast TV*, which meant leaving home at 6.30 am, with interviews throughout the day until *Newsnight* at 10.30 or later. In the invervals my wife was opening the letters which poured in like an avalanche, and I was trying to send them some kind of an answer, in addition to my ordinary constituency work, and, as far as I possibly could, carrying out my ordinary parliamentary duties. Looking back on it, it was all a blur. I remember being caught by *Sky TV* as I arrived at 6.45 am at ITN, and attempting to do an interview on the pavement, only to be blasted out by ITN's air conditioning system blowing a gale in our faces; and moving to the opposite pavement, which promptly subsided into the drain below it. I remember also a very jolly, and very lengthy, phone-in programme on Greater London Radio with Clement Freud as the interviewer ('Our guest tonight is Sir Anthony Meyer who, in the recent contest for the leadership of the Conservative Party, came second'). It was well after midnight before my wife and I got out of that studio; and I remembered that there was no milk at home for breakfast. There is a shop in the Edgware Road which is open all night for groceries, so I called in. Needless to say, the shop is kept by an Asian. As I went to pay for my pint he took one look at me, 'If you are who I think you are, the very best of luck to you!'

Throughout the contest and afterwards my parliamentary colleagues, with astonishingly few exceptions, remained extremely friendly (though there is one distinguished lady Member who ostentatiously fetches her newspaper from her capacious handbag and spreads it over the table if I sit down opposite her in the dining room). Several senior Ministers went out of their way to show personal kindness. And the Prime Minister herself? I hope I have made it clear throughout this narrative that, although I sympathise neither with her outlook nor with her style, I retain a huge admiration for her sheer guts, and I harbour no feelings of resentment against her.

There is no truth whatever in the story carried in one tabloid newspaper that she once cut me dead after the Falklands affair. On the contrary, she has always behaved, as one would have expected, with the courtesy and correctness which is her way. I cannot pretend that we had a close relationship. I have to admit that I found her alarming as a table companion; for she would make occasional forays into the Members' dining room on nights when it was crowded, preceded by her PPS to scout out two empty places. There was one famous occasion when a senior Tory MP tried to lighten the somewhat tense atmosphere which usually ensued by telling a slightly risqué story. There was an icy silence; and he is still waiting for the knighthood to which his years of service surely entitle him. My own experience of such encounters was not much happier. It was back in 1982, when we were making the first in our series of reforms in trade union law. I ventured the opinion that we should be careful not to alienate moderate trade union leaders. The blue eyes flashed, 'There is no such thing as a moderate trade union leader.' End of polite conversation.

After the contest I was asked if I had had any conversation with Mrs Thatcher; others have suggested that it would have been a good idea for her to have had me round for a drink afterwards to show that there were no hard feelings. Of course she didn't do this; and frankly she would not have been true to herself had she done so.

The result of the ballot on 5 December was such as to give satisfaction to everyone. The Prime Minister won a resounding victory; I got about twice as many votes as I had dared hope for. The total of votes for me plus abstentions was somewhat higher than I had expected, somewhat lower than I had hoped.

What did astonish me was the size of my mail. I received over 3,000 letters of support, and about 300 of disapproval. A very high proportion of the supportive letters began, 'I have been a Conservative all my life, but . . .' or, 'I was a very strong admirer of Mrs Thatcher until . . .' Many went on to say, 'Thank God at least someone has stood up to be counted.'

# CHAPTER SIXTEEN

# Deselection and After . . .

## January 1990

Now I had to face the music in my constituency, and in the local Conservative Association. The constituency was no problem; wherever we went people dashed across the road to shake hands with my wife and me and to express their support.

The Conservative Association was another matter. I had a long-standing commitment to address a meeting of the Executive Committee on 11 December. It was a rowdy, rather disorderly affair, quite like the House of Commons at Prime Minister's Question Time. It was clear that I had the support of one-quarter of the audience at most – and they were the silent quarter. Very wisely the chairman played for time, and announced that she would call a meeting of all paid-up members of the Conservative Association as soon as possible, which would be in mid January. Many of those present felt cheated; they had wanted to pass a vote of censure there and then; and the meeting broke up in disorder, much to the joy of the TV cameras.

It was only a reprieve. After the Christmas break (sliding

down some rather icy artificial snow at Courchevel), I was once again face to face with my accusers – this time all the paid-up members of the Clwyd North West Conservative Association. All the paid-up members turned out to be some 300 – out of 24,000 people who had voted Conservative in the constituency at the last election! I cannot pretend that I had made it especially easy for those who wanted to give me lenient treatment on account of my good record as a constituency member. I made it quite plain that I had no regrets for anything I had done, and that I intended to go on in exactly the same way as before. I was genuinely sorry if this was awkward for those who believed that it was the first duty of an MP to follow the party line, and to reflect the views of his own Conservative Association; but that I could no more be other than I am than could Mrs Thatcher.

I thought that it would be a close shave; and I admit that I was surprised, though not dismayed, when the vote was 2 to 1 against me. I made a gracious speech accepting the verdict, assured those of my friends who had voted against me that I still regarded them as my friends, and informed them all that I intended to go on being the MP, the very active Conservative MP for Clwyd North West.

Although a number of Conservative MPs have been deselected over the years, I am, I believe, the first to be deselected on political grounds since Nigel Nicolson was deselected at Bournemouth for his opposition to the Suez adventure; but I could not be charged, as he was charged, with neglecting my constituency, or being stand-offish. I doubt if any husband and wife teams have worked more assiduously than we have done, both throughout the constituency and with the local party organisation.

I have no doubt that the 200 party workers who voted against me did so with no personal animosity and with the conviction that they were doing a good job for the Party. I am not sure that would be the general verdict. It certainly does not seem to have been the verdict of the general body of electors in Clwyd North West who, in a poll conducted soon afterwards by HTV, condemned the decision to deselect me by a majority of four to one.

When I spoke at the meeting on 19 January I asked, 'What will the public say if you reject me tonight? Will they say, "And thus perish all traitors"? Or will they say, "What has happened to this Party, which used to pride itself on its tolerance of the broad spread of opinion within its ranks?"?'

Two hundred members of the Clwyd North West Conservative Association gave their answer to that question; it was that there is no room for dissent within the Party. The Leader is right all the time, and it is not for mere Party members to ask awkward questions. Our job is to help the Prime Minister to ram her policies down the throats of the British people. However, I do not believe that these policies, either at home or abroad, are any longer what the people want or what are in their best long-term interests. And I do not believe that she is capable of adjusting her policies to meet the new mood of the people, or their needs for the next century.

In an article which attracted some attention at the time, I described her as a woman of dauntless courage and meagre generosity; of commanding intellect and limited understanding; and I added that she is turning the Conservative Party into an intolerant, small-minded party in her own image.

I do not think that is an unfair assessment. It was a genuine attempt to present a balanced picture; but the concept of balance is out of favour in Mrs Thatcher's Conservative Party, as John Biffen found to his cost when he argued in favour of a 'balanced ticket', and promptly got the sack, having been the best Leader of the House of Commons in living memory.

But for Margaret Thatcher, he that is not with me is against me. If you are not 'One of Us' you are an enemy. And she seems to rejoice in making enemies. Her declaration after the Commonwealth Conference in Kuala Lumpur, that she felt sorry for the forty-seven who did not accept her stand on the lifting of South African sanctions, is revealing.

I remember standing on a station platform at Stresa just before World War II, and seeing a very ancient steam engine with a tall funnel puff noisily into the station, plastered with fascist emblems, and bearing on its antique funnel the chalked slogan '*Molti Nemici, Molto Onore*' – the more enemies the better. Mrs Thatcher's attitude is not so comically absurd as this; but she has managed to quarrel, and to keep her quarrel alive, with the churches (all the churches), the BBC most of the time and the IBA much of the time, the doctors, the nurses, the teachers, the local authorities at all levels, all the member countries of the EEC and particularly with the Germans, and still more particularly with the European Commission and its President, with every country in the Commonwealth and particularly with Canada, Australia and New Zealand, not forgetting the Scots, the Irish and the Welsh. It has to be said that she still has staunch support in the USA, the Soviet Union and South Africa.

It is hard to think of a better instance of her conviction that if everyone is against her she must be right, and must press on harder, than the story of the poll tax.

The poll tax was the one alternative to the unpopular rating system which was rejected out of hand by everyone who gave the matter serious thought. Kenneth Baker toyed with it, presumably as a top-up for some other method of financing local government. He like everyone else was attracted by the idea of making people realise that the items of local expenditure, the sports centres, the nursery classes, the public gardens, for which they vote so cheerfully have got to be paid for. No one could quarrel with this idea. But to make this flat-rate tax, which takes no account whatever of an individual's income or his living accommodation, into the sole source of locally raised revenue is so eccentric as to be of doubtful sanity. Lucky Kenneth Baker; he managed to move on to another Department before the obvious impossibility of translating the idea into practice became evident. It fell to Nicholas Ridley to try to implement the daft scheme. Ridley may be the ultimate Thatcher loyalist, but he is a highly intelligent and sensitive human being. He made little secret of his distaste for the unattractive and incontinent brat which had been deposited on his doorstep. Now it is for poor Chris Patten to find out how seriously his chances of eventually winning the leadership will be damaged by having to put this unworkable scheme into practice.

With his knowledge of political history he will no doubt reflect ruefully on the consequences which flowed from the last attempt to impose a tax which public opinion refused to accept as fair, and which excited widespread refusal to pay. In 1902 Prime Minister Balfour attempted to finance much needed improvements in secondary education by a levy on the rates. This was not a flat-rate tax, and it was for a generally accepted item of expenditure. But it involved nonconformist ratepayers contributing to the support of denominational schools; and it led to a massive campaign of civil disobedience. By the time the campaign ended there had been some 80,000 summonses for non-payment, and some 200 people had been sent to prison. The protest was on nothing like the scale or the intensity of the anti-poll tax campaign; but it contributed much to the Tories' landslide defeat in 1906.

But no such considerations will deflect Mrs Thatcher. This is the sort of issue which divides the men from the boys.

Maybe the British people don't like it, maybe they think it is unfair. Like it or not, fair or unfair, they are going to have it, and, in the end, they will grow to love it.

As she drives her party and the country towards the brick wall at the end of the road, Mrs Thatcher is in no mood to listen to the passengers urging her to use the brake or to turn the steering wheel. *She* knows that it is not really a brick wall, just a painted screen. Her foot is firmly on the accelerator.

That is why it is so important the Conservative Party find itself a new leader, if that can possibly be done; and to do so in time to win the next election. By far the best way for this to happen would be for Mrs Thatcher herself to step down before the end of the year. If she did she would depart in glory. The difficulties of the past few months would quickly be forgotten; and she would go down in history as one of Britain's most effective and significant prime ministers.

I have made no secret of my hope that Michael Heseltine will succeed her. I am quite certain that he is the Tory leader most likely to win the next election for us; he has flair, charisma and vision. I am almost equally certain that he will be a successful Prime Minister. I am by no means an uncritical admirer. I am not attracted by his flamboyance and his macho strutting on the defence stage. But the queries raised about the soundness of his judgement are wide of the mark; Winston Churchill made a greater number of more serious errors of judgement before he became Prime Minister, notably in his attitude towards Indian Home Rule and the abdication of Edward VIII. Nor do I go along with the criticism of his failure to show his hand in the matter of the leadership. If Heseltine is to lead a united party to victory he cannot be the one to challenge the present leader. It is true that once the contest is over the party unites behind its new leader with dramatic speed, as it did behind Mrs Thatcher when she destroyed

Edward Heath. But that was when the party was in opposition, and immediately after a second election defeat. Circumstances today are very different, and Heseltine has no choice
but to hold his hand and indicate his readiness to serve if
wanted.

Is there any possible alternative to Heseltine? Norman
Tebbit certainly has the talent, and the charisma. But I am
quite sure that a large number of Conservatives on the left
and in the centre of the Party could not accept him. The more
credible name being put forward by those who want to slow
up the Heseltine bandwagon is that of Douglas Hurd. Douglas
was a notably humane and successful Home Secretary; I have
no doubt that he will prove an outstanding Foreign Secretary
if Mrs Thatcher will allow him to get on with the job, or if he
can force her to let him. If he is going to force her, however,
he must be going to do so by stealth; there is as yet no
evidence that he is prepared to face her down.

I fear that dear Geoffrey Howe is no longer a serious
contestant; he has been worsted too often. Kenneth Clarke
still bears the bruises of his encounter with the medical
profession; Kenneth Baker is now, I fear, the grinning face of
Thatcherism.

Mrs Thatcher herself has made it clear that she wants her
eventual successor to come from the ranks of the next generation. If she gets her way, and is able to hand over to a
successor of her choice some time in the mid-1990s, it may
well be to some as yet unknown figure. But the two names
which figure in current speculation are Chris Patten and John
Major.

Chris Patten has some very strong support, notably among
some members of the Whips' Office. Indeed, one of the very
few MPs who tried to exert real pressure on me during the

leadership contest was a fairly senior Whip who was concerned that by precipitating a premature contest I was spoiling Patten's chances. Chris, poor fellow, will have to carry the heavy cross of the poll tax on his back for some time to come; but I have a feeling that he will contrive to slip out from under it more deftly than Ken Clarke has been able to escape the falling masonry of the NHS reforms.

John Major is the great unknown. All we know is that he is a man of quite extraordinary modesty and kindness, invariably courteous to his political opponents (which makes a nice change from Mrs Thatcher's abrasive ways), and immensely skilled at whatever task he undertakes. If all these virtues suffice, then he will make a great leader. But does he have the fire, and does he have the steel?

My choice is for Heseltine. I accept that it is not practicable for him to challenge Mrs Thatcher directly. But some challenge there must be. In the meantime I have a job to do.

# CHAPTER SEVENTEEN

# Still Very Much
# a Tory

## 1990 and Beyond

Party workers, for whatever party, are people who have no room for doubt about either the policies or the leadership of their party. If they were the sort of people who afford themselves the luxury of doubt, then they would not be the sort of people who are ready to go out in all weather knocking on doors, delivering leaflets, collecting subscriptions, or, more testing still, defending the sometimes unpopular policies of their party in the bus queue or at the bar counter. It is easy enough to sneer at them for having closed minds. They are, in fact, the salt of the earth; and our democracy would be a sickly plant without them and their devotion. Every MP knows how much he owes, and how much our free society owes, to the untiring, unthanked efforts of these, the poor bloody infantry of democracy. When I started out in politics I had the idea that the floating voter was the intelligent, thoughtful chap one had to try to convert. Of course there are floating voters of this sort; but the great majority of floating voters are people who decide which candidate they are going to vote for by the colour of his eyes, or some such totally frivolous reason. Just as the party worker does far more to preserve democracy then the most sagacious of political pundits, so the loyal party supporter is likely to be a worthier and more intelligent chap than the voter who changes his party at each election.

The party workers recognise this; and it is striking how well the workers of the different parties get on with one another when they are thrown together, as they are at an election count.

Party workers, having no room or time for doubt themselves, naturally look to their candidate or MP, whom they regard as their leader however hard he may seek to disclaim the title, to proclaim the Party's policies with all the eloquence and force that he, as a trained politician, is expected to possess. When things are going well for the Party a certain measure of dissent is acceptable, provided that it is directed away from the centre; that is to say, it is all right for Conservative MPs to express views which are to the right of the party line, and for Labour MPs to wander off to the left; but woe betide those who stray towards the middle. And woe betide those who step out of line when the Party is in danger. When that happens, the party workers expect everyone to close ranks; and, if things get bad enough, to root out the traitors and faint-hearts and expel them.

It was therefore neither surprising nor deplorable that my local Conservative Association should have decided to deselect me. I cannot possibly blame them. Among those who voted against me were, I feel pretty sure, many whom I regard as personal friends; for one does develop many close ties of friendship with one's party workers, as with many others within one's constituency. But I do question the political wisdom of their decision. I know that it is awkward to have an MP who is forever questioning the policies which you, a loyal party worker, are trying to put over to the voter on the doorstep as the rain from the porch runs down your neck and your bunch of election literature dissolves into blue slurry. I know too that the Conservative Party differs slightly from the Labour Party in attaching a mystical value to party loyalty. But I do not believe that the great voting public attaches anywhere near the same value to this display of loyalty. On the contrary, I believe that the electorate are now sufficiently mature to prefer a party where there is evidence of lively internal debate, even on a subject so sacrosanct as the leadership.

In short I believe that by deselecting me in January 1990, the Clwyd North West Conservative Association, so far from strengthening the Conservative Party by this purge, actually weakened it by giving a display of narrow-minded intolerance. That certainly seemed to be the clear message given by an opinion poll conducted in March 1990, which showed not only a 3 to 1 majority against my deselection, but which also showed that without me as candidate the seat would be lost to Labour; and that, were I to stand as an independent Conservative, I would beat the official Conservative candidate into third place and win the seat myself quite comfortably.

One of the few critical letters which appeared in the local paper said that I was a good MP, but that I was in the wrong party. That is the charge which I want to meet by way of a conclusion.

It is true that I am profoundly and increasingly unhappy about many of the Conservative Party's policies, and about the style and outlook of our present leader. I want to see a Conservative Party which is always aware of its duty to all our people, rich and poor, black and white, young and old; and a Party ready to take up the challenging role which awaits us in Europe, east as well as west.

But a Conservative I am, and a Conservative I remain. If the Conservative Party does not have room for people like me in it, then its chances of retaining power and providing the future Government of this country are hugely reduced, for it cannot go on winning purely on the votes of unquestioning Conservatives. In any case the Conservative Party for the past 150 years has been much closer to the kind of ideas that I uphold than to those which have held sway for the past ten years.

Why am I a Conservative? Because I believe that only the Conservative Party can sustain a government through the tough decisions which have to be taken in the course of day-to-day administration, let alone at moments of great crisis.

Only a Conservative Government, supported by the Conservative Party, will give that overriding priority to the process of wealth creation, without which the glib promises of fairer shares are cynical swindles. Only a Conservative Government, sustained by the Conservative Party, will ensure that the defence of this country gets the share of national resources which it needs to carry out its task against the competing claims of other, more popular items of expenditure.

Only a Conservative Government, sustained by the Conservative Party, will give that unequivocal backing to the forces of order which is needed if the rule of law is to be put beyond question.

I am not one of those party politicians who believes that my party is always right, and the other party always wrong. But I really do believe that the Labour Party will always be tempted to pursue the redistribution of wealth to the point where its creation is endangered; that it will never be fully free of the influence of those who would strip our country of effective defence, either because they cannot imagine an enemy with aggressive intention or because they grudge the expenditure; and that its devotion to the rule of law is at risk from those within its ranks who hold to the concept that unjust laws may be legitimately disobeyed, and from those who uphold the right of industrial action for political ends. I know that the great majority of Labour Party members are patriotic, law-abiding citizens; but the party has a larger and more influential element which is outside the broad consensus of national interest than is to be found in the Conservative Party.

For those reasons I am, and I will remain, a Conservative, even if a frequently nonconformist one. And, for the avoidance of doubt, I am, and I intend to remain, the Conservative Member of Parliament for Clwyd North West for some time to come.